Teaching and Assessing Intercultural Communicative Competence

Multilingual Matters

Cric Crac! Teaching and Learning French through Storytelling
ROY DUNNING
Distance Education for Language Teachers
RON HOWARD and IAN McGRATH (eds)
Effective Language Learning
SUZANNE GRAHAM
The Elements of Foreign Language Teaching
WALTER GRAUBERG
French for Communication 1979-1990
ROY DUNNING
Inspiring Innovations in Language Teaching
JUDITH HAMILTON
The Good Language Learner
N. NAIMAN, M. FRÖHLICH, H.H. STERN and A. TODESCO
Le ou La? The Gender of French Nouns
MARIE SURRIDGE
Second Language Practice
GEORGES DUQUETTE (ed.)
Target Language, Collaborative Learning and Autonomy
ERNESTO MACARO
Teacher Education for LSP
RON HOWARD and GILLIAN BROWN (eds)
Validation in Language Testing
A. CUMMING and R. BERWICK (eds)

Please contact us for the latest book information:
Multilingual Matters Ltd, Frankfurt Lodge, Clevedon Hall,
Victoria Road, Clevedon, England, BS21 7HH

Teaching and Assessing Intercultural Communicative Competence

Michael Byram

MULTILINGUAL MATTERS LTD
Clevedon • Philadelphia • Toronto • Sydney • Johannesburg

Library of Congress Cataloging in Publication Data

Byram, Michael
Teaching and Assessing Intercultural Communicative Competence/Michael Byram
Includes bibliographical references and index
1. Language and languages–Study and teaching. 2. Multicultural education.
3. Intercultural communication–Study and teaching. 4. Communicative competence.
I. Title.
P53.45.B96 1997
418'.007–dc21 97-6559

British Library Cataloguing in Publication Data

A CIP catalogue record for this book is available from the British Library.

ISBN 1-85359-387-8 (hbk)
ISBN 1-85359-377-X (pbk)

Multilingual Matters Ltd

UK: Frankfurt Lodge, Clevedon Hall, Victoria Road, Clevedon BS21 7HH.
USA: 1900 Frost Road, Suite 101, Bristol, PA 19007, USA.
Canada: OISE, 712 Gordon Baker Road, Toronto, Ontario, Canada M2H 3R7.
Australia: P.O. Box 586, Artamon, NSW, Australia.
South Africa: PO Box 1080, Northcliffe 2115, Johannesburg, South Africa.

Contents

Preface

Although I am the sole author of this monograph and take responsibility for what it says, it owes much to its origins in a particular project and to the people involved. I am above all grateful to Geneviève Zarate, with whom I have enjoyed the privilege of co-operation and joint authorship for several years. She may not agree with all that I say but her ideas have profoundly influenced this text.

In 1989 in *Cultural Studies in Foreign Language Education,* I wrote that one of the areas crucially in need of further research was the assessment of the cultural dimension in language learning. I was therefore very pleased to be invited to participate in the Council of Europe's project to develop a 'Common European Framework of Reference for Language Learning and Teaching'. The Framework was to be based on definitions of levels of proficiency in the use of languages, and Geneviève Zarate and I were invited to write a paper to clarify the issues involved in determining levels of 'socio-cultural competence'.

The paper, 'Definitions, objectives and assessment of socio-cultural competence' was written to a tight schedule. This had the advantage of obliging us to formulate our thinking quickly and clearly, and the disadvantage of allowing little time for reflection, revision or elaboration. It also meant that the formulation was related to a particular model of language learning and to other position papers in the project.

It is possible that without the stimulus of the Council of Europe project, we would not have put pen to paper or hand to computer, being too wary of the complexities of the issues. For me, it served as a significant first step, whose direction was determined by writing together with Geneviève Zarate. Research Fellowships in Durham and Washington DC, provided the second stimulus and the intellectual and physical space in which to pursue the ideas of our original paper. This time the purpose and the readership is different. My hope is that this monograph will be accessible to anyone interested in foreign language teaching and learning, whatever the context in which they live and work. I realise that I am setting myself a difficult task because language teaching and learning are social phenomena differing according to time and place. Assessment in particular is linked to societal demands, to ensure quality of education, to plan for national needs, to facilitate mobility, and so on. To say anything useful for every context is difficult but important, partly for reasons internal to the field, and partly because national concerns are now being complemented by international ones.

I referred above to the different origins and contexts in which this monograph has been produced. At the Council of Europe, I am particularly grateful to Antonietta de Vigili, Joe Shiels and John Trim.

At the National Foreign Language Center, I was very fortunate in being in residence with Ross Steele and Myriam Met, who were generous with their time in reading my long-hand script, and stimulating in discussion of my ill-formed first drafts. It was also a novel and rewarding experience, on my first visit to the United States, to be coping with new cultural practices, a whole range of cultures, and attempting to communicate in a language in which I was a proficient foreigner, whilst at the same time retiring to the haven of my office to write about the 'intercultural speaker'. Theory and practice were one.

I am grateful to the University of Durham for the award of a Sir Derman Christophersen Research Fellowship, and to the National Foreign Language Center at the Johns Hopkins University, Washington DC for the award of an Andrew Mellon Fellowship. It was a pleasure to be a colleague of David Maxwell, his staff and other visiting Fellows — particularly my neighbours Mats Oscarrson and Stephen Straight — for three months.

I would also like to acknowledge the helpful comments on a draft of the manuscript by an anonymous reviewer who provided encouragement and detailed suggestions for improvements.

I am grateful to Susan Metcalfe who patiently and efficiently typed my first draft, written still with paper and pencil, I have to confess.

As always, my wife, Marie Thérèse, allowed me the luxury of quiet essential for writing, and put up with my absences, whilst my attention was elsewhere. My best, and best-loved examples of 'intercultural speakers' are our children Alice and Ian, who are an inspiration.

Michael Byram
Durham, January 1997

Introduction

The Tourist and the Sojourner

The purpose of this monograph is to explore the issues which arise if we wish to evaluate and/or assess a person's ability to relate to and communicate with people who speak a different language and live in a different cultural context. The need to do this is not a new one. Relationships between different cultural and linguistic groups are at the heart of diplomacy and the need to choose appropriate ambassadors of one group to another is as old as civilised societies. What is new, however, is the condition of the world which allows and encourages all the people in a cultural and linguistic group, not just its diplomats and professional travellers, to take up contact with people in other groups. This happens in two quite different ways, making for the people involved two quite different roles: that of the tourist and that of the sojourner.

The role of the tourist — and the word itself — is far more familiar than the word and characteristics of the sojourner, for the latter has touched fewer people hitherto, at least in Western societies. In the West, it has been the fate only of small numbers of the social elite but of much larger groups of people of low social status, especially migrant labourers, from non-Western countries. The tourist, on the other hand, is a role taken by very large numbers of all social classes in Western countries, and has been so for almost fifty years — anticipated by the enforced 'tourism' affecting many people in the 1939–1945 war who would otherwise never have left their region, let alone their country. However, although tourism has had major economic consequences, it is the sojourner who produces effects on a society which challenge its unquestioned and unconscious beliefs, behaviours and meanings, and whose own beliefs, behaviours and meanings are in turn challenged and expected to change. The tourist hopes for quite the opposite effect, first that what they have travelled to see will not change, for otherwise the journey would lose its purpose, and second that their own way of living will be enriched but not fundamentally changed by the experience of seeing others.

The experience of the sojourner is one of comparisons, of what is the same or different but compatible, but also of conflicts and incompatible contrasts. The experience of the sojourner is potentially more valuable than that of the tourist, both for societies and for individuals, since the state of the world is such that societies and individuals have no alternative but proximity, interaction and relationship as the conditions of existence. Societies benefit from more harmonious co-existence, and individuals gain an understanding of others and of themselves which makes them more conscious of their humanity and more able to reflect upon and question the social conditions in which they live. Where the tourist remains essentially unchanged, the sojourner has the opportunity to learn and be educated, acquiring the capacity to critique and improve their own and others' conditions.

Teaching and Assessment

Yet why evaluate and assess the qualities of a sojourner? Is it not enough to let these qualities emerge and to create the conditions propitious for societal harmony and individual education? The answer lies at one level in the institutions in which the qualities are developed, but also in the underlying characteristics of social groups and societies.

Social groups informally, and societies through their formal institutions, have as a first priority their own longevity and they ensure that their members acquire loyalty and group identity from an early age. Their institutions support this through processes of socialisation, particularly in educational institutions, but at the same time, schools and other educational institutions are also increasingly expected to prepare those entrusted to them for the inter-lingual and inter-cultural experiences of the contemporary world. For the qualities of the sojourner, which run counter to the many influences creating a sense of loyalty and group identity, are seldom acquired without help, are seldom learnt without teaching. Educational institutions therefore have a responsibility, and a need to demonstrate their ability to fulfil it, to show they are accountable. Evaluation of their general efficacy, and assessment of the individuals in their charge are part of that accountability, and also serve the individuals in providing them with certification of their capacities, a certification which enables them to gain acceptance as sojourners in another society.

Evaluation and assessment cannot and should not be separate from the teaching and general institutional arrangements, and it is therefore inevitable that this monograph should deal with teaching as well as assessment of individuals. On the other hand it will not deal with evaluation of general arrangements, of the efficacy of the realisation of plans and principles for teaching and assessment. It will focus on the principles, on the ways in which they can inform planning and on the relationship between teaching and assessment.

Intercultural Communicative Competence

The qualities required of the sojourner are what I shall label 'intercultural communicative competence' (ICC). The phrase deliberately maintains a link with recent traditions in foreign language teaching, but expands the concept of 'communicative competence' in significant ways. The link makes it explicit that our focus will be on the contribution of foreign language teaching (FLT) to the development of the qualities required of a sojourner, although there are other areas within schools and other educational institutions which can also contribute. FLT should not and does not need to claim sole responsibility for the teaching and assessment of ICC. Other subject areas such as geography or the teaching of literature can introduce learners to other worlds and the experience of otherness. History can confront learners with otherness in the dimension of time. FLT however has the experience of otherness at the centre of its concern, as it requires learners to engage with both familiar and unfamiliar experience through the medium of another language. Furthermore, FLT has a central aim of enabling learners to use that language to interact with people for whom it is their preferred and 'natural' medium of experience, those we call 'native speakers', as well as in lingua franca situations where it is an estranging and sometimes disturbing means of coping with the world for all concerned.

FLT is therefore concerned with communication but this has to be understood as more than the exchange of information and sending of messages, which has dominated 'communicative language teaching' in recent years. Even the exchange of information is dependent upon understanding how what one says or writes will be perceived and interpreted in another cultural context; it depends on the ability to decentre and take up the perspective of the listener or reader. But successful 'communication' is not judged solely in terms of the efficiency of information exchange. It is focused on establishing and maintaining relationships. In this sense, the efficacy of communication depends upon using language to demonstrate one's willingness to relate, which often involves the indirectness of politeness rather than the direct and 'efficient' choice of language full of information. That ways of being polite vary from one language and culture to another is widely known, but this is often reduced to the acquisition of particular formulae. Politeness is however only the visible symptom of a more complex phenomenon: the differences in beliefs, behaviours and meanings through which people interact with each other, differences which may be incompatible and contain the seeds of conflict unless relationships are maintained through politeness.

The introduction of the language of politeness into syllabi for communicative language teaching, for example in the revised version of the Council of Europe's *'Threshold Level'* (van Ek & Trim, 1991) is a sign of change. Communication is being presented as interaction among people of complex cultural and social identities. FLT needs to be based on such syllabi but also to go beyond linguistic realisations of politeness to take account of the ways of living out of which others speak and write. Only then can FLT claim to prepare learners to communicate and interact with foreigners who are 'other' and accepted as such, rather than being reduced to people assumed to be (almost) 'like us'.

Teaching and Assessing ICC: A Framework

It follows from the view of communication and interaction presented here that it is specific combinations of individuals with specific cultural identities which are the outcome of FLT. There can be no generalisable syllabus, neither linguistic nor cultural. A French learner of English needs a different syllabus and methods to a Greek, and different again from a Japanese, and within each of these national groups there are different needs arising from age, purpose, institution and so on. Similarly the assessment of their success as learners needs to take account of specific learners' origins as well as the languages and cultures they are learning. It is therefore inevitable that non-specific discussion can provide only a framework, a discussion of principles, illustrated with specific examples, but no more.

The framework offered in this monograph is an attempt to clarify principles which give adequate recognition to the view of FLT presented briefly above. It is written above all from the FLT perspective and has a strong link to the teaching of foreign languages in general education. It is thus written particularly for FLT professionals, be they teachers or policy makers or language planners. I considered writing the text in such a way that it would also include Second Language Teaching, i.e. the teaching of a language which is routinely spoken outside the classroom in the society in which the learner lives. There are clearly significant similarities between FLT and SLT, and the distinction is not a dichotomous one, but rather a question of degree. However it is precisely this complexity which decided me against trying to take the variety of factors into consideration throughout the text. It would have otherwise been full of digressions and qualifications to cover a range of cases. The intention is to write at a level of abstraction which can be related to FLT or SLT in a wide range of situations, although it is necessary to use specific examples and terminology. Thus I shall refer to foreign countries and societies where I might also have referred to communities with a second language within a learner's own country. It would be tedious to try to formulate the text in such a way that it refers to all possibilities, and I hope readers who consider themselves to be involved in SLT will make their own amendments and qualifications and still find the text useful.

A text of this kind, which attempts to discuss general principles, is difficult to make accessible to all the readers one would wish. It has to be positioned at a high level of abstraction if it is to be valid in its claims, yet this tends to create difficulties in following the argument. Constantly to offer examples, however, can cause clutter and even lead readers to reject the argument because a particular example does not hold in their situation. I have tried to compromise by offering some examples but not exemplifying every point. The monograph will perhaps function best when used in teacher education, where readers can discuss the argument with respect to their own concrete situation, rather than hypothetical illustrations which I might provide. I would nonetheless wish to assure readers that the text arises out of my own experience of concrete situations over many years of teaching and teacher education.

Chapter 1 sets the scene by discussing the nature of intercultural competence and communication, and makes the point that FLT is an enterprise which always takes place in specific circumstances, is inevitably influenced by those circumstances and should be planned to suit the environment in which it takes place. In Chapter 2, I offer a descriptive model of intercultural communicative competence (ICC). This is a description of the components which contribute to the ability to understand and relate to people from other countries, and is intended to be a comprehensive and rich description of what is required in the most complex and also the most favourable circumstances of intercultural communication. It is not a blueprint for all FLT. Since FLT has to be responsive to its environment, it is frequently the case that FLT quite properly does not attempt to develop in learners the most complex competence possible.

Chapters 3 and 4 take the discussion closer to the immediate concerns of FLT professionals. In Chapter 3, I formulate the description of ICC in terms of objectives. These provide a means of determining what the teacher and learner wish to achieve by suggesting what knowledge, behaviour, skill or attitude might 'count as' a part of ICC. Chapter 4 considers how these objectives might also be used to plan a curriculum, and is therefore intended to be particularly useful in setting the parameters within which FLT takes place on a routine basis.

Chapter 5 is intended for those who are involved in the assessment of

FLT, which has traditionally focused on the testing of linguistic competence. Even though policy statements commonly claim that the aims of FLT include knowledge of other countries, changes in attitudes to foreign languages and peoples, and so on, assessment of the degree to which individual learners achieve those aims and evaluation of the success of programmes of study in helping to do so, have taken place very rarely. It is often said that such assessment is not possible, or not reliable or valid enough to be used when learners are to be given certification of their abilities. Yet it is also commonly observed that the lack of assessment leads to insufficient attention to teaching processes which can help learners to achieve what is, after all, a central dimension of FLT. Chapter 5 addresses these issues by discussing the assessment options for the objectives proposed in earlier chapters. It argues that objective testing is perhaps necessary in some circumstances, but insufficient to reflect the full complexity of intercultural communicative competence. Other approaches which relate teaching and assessment more closely need to be developed.

Chapter 1

Defining and Describing Intercultural Communicative Competence

Introduction

The assessment of an individual's ability to communicate and interact across cultural boundaries is facilitated by a detailed description of the process involved and definition of what is expected of the individual. It is an advantage to the assessor but also to both teacher and learner. All three can benefit from clarity and transparency (Council of Europe, 1993: 5) and agree upon the aims and purposes of the teaching, learning and assessment processes in which they are involved. It is important to remember, too, that their aims and purposes are determined in part by the societal contexts in which they find themselves — national, international and intra-national — and by the preoccupations of institutions, which reflect those of the societies in which they function.

In this first chapter, I shall begin to describe and define Intercultural Communicative Competence (ICC) as it relates to foreign language teaching. This will involve building up a view of ICC from a base in existing FLT theory, and adding to it insights from other disciplines, in order to offer a model of ICC capable of informing discussion of teaching and assessment. I shall however also consider how that model relates to some specific contexts, to illustrate the general need always to define models of ICC according to the requirements of the situations in which learners find themselves.[1]

Communicating Across Linguistic and Cultural Boundaries

Communicative competence

The concept 'communicative competence' was developed in the anglophone world by Hymes' critique of Chomsky and in the germanophone literature by Habermas.[2] Hymes argued that linguists wishing to understand first language acquisition, need to pay attention to the way in which not only grammatical competence but also the ability to use language appropriately is acquired. He thus put emphasis on sociolinguistic competence and this concept was fundamental to the development of communicative language teaching, when Hymes' description of first language acquisition and communication among native speakers was transferred into the description of the aims and objectives of foreign language teaching and learning. I shall argue later that this transfer is misleading because it implicitly suggests that foreign language learners should model themselves on first language speakers, ignoring the significance of the social identities and cultural competence of the learner in any intercultural interaction. In fact, Hymes' argument ought to lead to a greater awareness of the relationship between linguistic and sociocultural competence, since he described linguistic competence as just one kind of cultural competence:

> From a finite experience of speech acts and their interdependence with sociocultural features, (children) develop a general theory of speaking appropriate in their community which they employ, *like other forms of tacit cultural knowledge* (competence) in conducting and interpreting social life. (my emphasis)
>
> ...
>
> From a communicative standpoint, judgements of appropriateness may not be assigned to different spheres, as between the linguistic and the cultural; certainly the spheres of the two will interact. (Hymes, 1972: 279, 286)

However, in the following decade, in his major review of language teaching Stern argued that the sociolinguistic might have developed but that the sociocultural had not:

> As a generalisation, one can say that language teaching theory is fast acquiring a sociolinguistic component but still lacks a well-defined socio-cultural emphasis. (Stern, 1983: 246)

This was the case in the 1980s and into the 1990s. For example, even in the work of the Council of Europe, the socio-cultural component was not dealt with as thoroughly as the sociolinguistic (van Ek, 1986) until a new version of the Threshold Level was produced (van Ek & Trim, 1991) and a Framework of reference for language learning and teaching introduced a more nuanced vision (Council of Europe, 1996).

The reasons for this diversion from cultural knowledge/competence are yet to be clarified but Roberts (forthcoming) has argued that what has happened is that the link with the cultural sphere has been lost because, despite the origins in Hymes, language teaching has been influenced above all by speech act theory and discourse analysis, where the linguistic predominates.

Hymes was not writing for the FLT profession and did not pay specific attention to cross-cultural communication; he was concerned to analyse social interaction and communication within a social group using one language. The interpretation of the concept for FLT was undertaken by others, in North America by Canale & Swain (1980) and in Europe by van Ek (1986), working independently of each other. The former developed their work from Hymes and others. van Ek makes no explicit reference to either Hymes or Habermas, but presented his work as part of a developing project under the auspices of the Council of Europe; in fact, van Ek refers to 'communicative ability'. The work of Canale and Swain and van Ek and the Council of Europe team has much in common and could be analysed comparatively. I propose here however to take van Ek's work as a starting point, partly because it is more detailed and partly because it was the origin of the model I shall present later.[3]

van Ek presents what he calls 'a framework for comprehensive foreign language learning objectives' (1986: 33) which is explicitly developed in the context of his view of how FLT must be justified through its contribution to learners' general education. He emphasises that FLT is not just concerned with training in communication skills but also with the personal and social development of the learner as an individual. His framework thus includes reference to 'social competence', 'the promotion of autonomy' and the 'development of social responsibility' which are perhaps inherent in the original discussions of communicative competence but certainly not central and explicit. Nor are they part of the interpretation of communicative competence undertaken by Canale and Swain. Yet, as I suggested earlier, the institutional context in which ICC is taught cannot be ignored, nor can a society's requirements of FL teachers, and I shall follow van Ek in framing the discussion within a general educational context.

There is no doubt however that the definition of communicative competence and ICC is made more complex by this contextualisation, as are the issues of assessment. For example, the assessment of autonomy or social responsibility might be not only technically complex but also involve significant ethical issues, concerning the right of an institution and its members to make judgements about an individual's degree of social responsibility. van Ek was not concerned with assessment — or methodology — but only with objectives and content. It may ultimately be appropriate to assess only part of what we define as ICC.

van Ek's model of 'communicative ability' (1986: 35) comprises six 'competences', together with autonomy and social responsibility. He emphasises that these are not discrete elements, but that they are different aspects of one concept (1986: 36). His approach is like someone observing a globe by circling around it and stopping at six points. At any one point, one aspect will be central but others, and their relationship to that aspect, will also be in view. This is an important and positive dimension of his approach. On the other hand there are still omissions and also a tendency to posit the native speaker communicating with other native speakers as the underlying phenomenon which the model has to describe, a tendency to retain the native speaker as a model for the learner, which I shall argue against later. The problem would be rendered even more complex if this were then retained for purposes of assessment too.

Nonetheless the model of six competences is a useful starting point and can be summarised as follows:

- *Linguistic competence*: the ability to produce and interpret meaningful utterances which are formed in accordance with the rules of the language concerned and bear their conventional meaning ... that meaning which native speakers would normally attach to an utterance when used in isolation (p. 39).
- *Sociolinguistic competence*: the awareness of ways in which the choice of language forms ... is determined by such conditions as setting, relationship between communication partners, communicative intention, etc., etc. ... sociolinguistic competence covers the relation between linguistic signals and their contextual — or situational — meaning (p. 41).
- *Discourse competence*: the ability to use appropriate strategies in the construction and interpretation of texts (p. 47).
- *Strategic competence*: when communication is difficult we have to find ways of 'getting our meaning across' or of 'finding out what somebody means'; these are communication strategies, such as rephrasing, asking for clarification (p. 55).
- *Socio-cultural competence*: every language is situated in a sociocultural context and implies the use of a particular reference frame which is partly different from that of the foreign language learner; socio-cultural competence presupposes a certain degree of familiarity with that context (p. 35).
- *Social competence*: involves both the will and the skill to interact with others, involving motivation, attitude, self-confidence, empathy and the ability to handle social situations (p. 65).

It is above all in linguistic and sociolinguistic competence that the native speaker as model is implicit in van Ek's definition. He requires learners to speak or write 'in accordance with the rules of the language concerned', without specifying the origins and nature of 'the rules'. He also requires utterances to 'bear their conventional meaning', i.e. 'that meaning which native speakers would normally attach to an utterance when used in isolation'. Even if this concept of 'use in isolation' has to be viewed with some concern — it is not possible to use an utterance isolated from all social contexts, even if the speaker is alone — it might be interpreted as the meanings defined in dictionaries. Yet in both cases the authority and evaluation of a learner's use is vested in the native speaker, not explicitly defined, but perhaps implicitly referring to the educated native speaker. Kramsch (1993, and in press) has argued for a quite different view, namely that the learner has rights to use a foreign language for their own purposes, and makes the very important point that van Ek's approach places power in social interaction in the hands of the native speaker.

With respect to 'sociocultural competence', there is again a tendency to view the learner as an incomplete native speaker. The definition refers to knowledge of the context 'in which that language is used by native speakers' and competence presupposes 'a certain degree' of familiarity with that context. Even in the case where the language is used as a lingua franca, although there will be 'least need' for sociocultural competence, nonetheless lingua franca speakers should 'be aware of *the* sociocultural implications of the language forms they are using' (1986: 63 — emphasis added). Again the implication of there being only one set of sociocultural implications for a language appears to refer to native speakers.

There are two kinds of reason for criticising the use of the native speaker as a model, in which van Ek is just one of many. The first is a pragmatic educational one which has been recognised widely in recent years. It is the problem of creating an impossible target and consequently inevitable failure. The requirement that learners have the same mastery over a language as an (educated) native speaker ignores the conditions under which learners and native speakers learn and acquire a language. I suspect it is linked to a belief that if bilinguals can speak two languages perfectly, then so can learners of a foreign language. This view is uninformed because it does not take into account the literature which shows that few if any bilinguals are 'perfect' in linguistic competence, even less so in sociolinguistic or sociocultural competence.

The second ground for criticism of the native speaker model is that, even were it possible, it would create the wrong kind of competence. It would imply that a learner should be linguistically schizophrenic, abandoning one language in order to blend into another linguistic environment, becoming accepted as a native speaker by other native speakers. This linguistic schizophrenia also suggests separation from one's own culture and the acquisition of a native sociocultural competence, and a new sociocultural identity. The strains involved in this process, even if it were desirable and possible, are related to the psychological stress of 'culture shock' (Furnham & Bochner, 1986) and could be permanently damaging (cf. Paulston (1992) for a personal description of 'being bicultural').

As I shall argue in more detail later, the more desirable outcome is a learner with the ability to see and manage the relationships between themselves and their own cultural beliefs, behaviours and meanings,[4] as expressed in a foreign language, and those of their interlocutors, expressed in the same language — or even a combination of languages — which may be the interlocutors' native language, or not. The value of van Ek's model is that it identifies a number of components or aspects of communicative and interactional ability for further analysis. It does so by taking a starting point in the analysis of where and how a foreign language might be used, rather than in the analysis of language isolated from use. It also takes into account the place where foreign languages are most widely taught — schools and other educational institutions — and their functions and goals in their society. However, complex though van Ek's analysis may be, it does not take into account all the social factors necessary for the analysis. The history of language teaching is the history of increasing understanding of the nature of language and the attempts to incorporate new discoveries into methods and objectives. There is no reason to believe that we have reached the end of that development. It is partly a function of changes in language use leading to changes in the nature of language, and therefore subject to yet further societal change. All we can do here is attempt to take analyses such as that by van Ek the further steps required by more recent discoveries.

An obvious direction for this work is to introduce discoveries related to van Ek's linguistic and sociolinguistic competences. More detailed analysis of the grammar of a language, for example, has implications for the specification of linguistic competence. On the other hand, there are other perspectives which are just as important and perhaps less familiar to the FLT profession, those related to sociocultural and social competence for example. It is these that we shall pursue here because they throw light on non-linguistic aspects of communication and on an understanding of communication as human interaction, not just as exchange of information.

Non-verbal communication

The first area is one which van Ek's analysis does not cover and which is seldom dealt with at more than a superficial level by FL teachers. In his classic discussion of *'The Psychology of Interpersonal Behaviour'*, Argyle (1983) identifies eight dimensions of non-verbal communication:

- facial expression;
- gaze;
- gestures and other bodily movements;
- bodily posture;
- bodily contact;
- spatial behaviour;
- clothes and appearance;
- non-verbal aspects of speech

and four functions in which these modes of non-verbal communication can operate:

- communicating interpersonal attitudes and emotions;
- self-presentation;
- rituals;
- supporting verbal communication.

He points out that there is variation in non-verbal communication between cultures and that 'when people from two different cultures meet, there is infinite scope for misunderstanding and confusion' (Argyle, 1983: 189). He deals briefly with the ways of overcoming such problems and suggests that language learning is a valuable but time-consuming approach to other cultures, as are modes of social skills learning which prepare people for contact with other cultures.

Poyatos (1992) addresses these issues very much from the perspective of the foreign language teacher, arguing that traditional FLT is too narrow in its concerns. Language teachers should be concerned with 'the triple reality of speech (language, paralanguage and kinesics)' and that these should be seen within a broader context of cultural signs of all kinds. He identifies ten dimensions of communication where the learner may meet problems, the first four of which are familiar to the language teacher, but are insufficient as a basis for intercultural communication:

- phonetics/phonemics;
- morphology;
- syntax;
- vocabulary;
- paralanguage (e.g. tongue clicks, meaningful use of loudness and whispering);
- kinesics (e.g. communicative gestures, manners and postures);

- proxemics (e.g. personal or intimate distances between peers, parents, acquaintances);
- chemical/dermal (e.g. tear-shedding, blushing);
- body-adaptors/object-adaptors (e.g. cosmetics, clothes, occupational artefacts);
- built and modified environments (e.g. status objects such as homes and gardens).

Poyatos then proposes an approach to determining a syllabus and a methodology for a course in non-verbal communication, dealing above all with the inter-relationships between language, paralanguage and kinesics.[5] Unlike Argyle, who acknowledges the difficulty of acquiring the modes of non-verbal communication of other cultures, Poyatos seems to assume that they can in fact be taught, together with or separate from verbal communication. Argyle suggests the alternative of skills and sensitivity training in view of the difficulty, but neither Argyle nor Poyatos question whether, as an ideal, the learner should attempt to acquire the non-verbal communication of a native speaker. Poyatos sees the problems of learning as including the reduction of 'interference' from the learner's own non-verbal system in order to imitate the native-speaker.

Yet precisely because many aspects of non-verbal communication, although learned within a given cultural environment, are unconscious, the language learner may not be able to control them, or wish to give up what feels like a part of their personality, to acquire the non-verbal communication of others. Here again, therefore, it is important that the learner be able to see similarities and difference and to establish a relationship between their own and other systems, rather than imitate a native-speaker.

Inter-group and cross-cultural relations

A second line of enquiry which may surprise FL teachers by its minimal concern for language, is the research into communication and interaction between groups, pursued by those who might be broadly described as cross-cultural psychologists. In an overview of 'the study of cross-cultural competence', Ruben emphasises how the work he is reviewing arises out of 'practical problems encountered by individuals living and working overseas, and by their institutional sponsors' (Ruben, 1989: 229). The problems are described in psychological terms and the general model he offers is dominated by skills in interpersonal relationships:

> (Cross-cultural) competence has various facets:
> (1) Relational-Building and Maintenance Competence: Competence

associated with the establishment and maintenance of positive relationships.

(2) Information-Transfer Competence: Competence associated with the transmission of information with minimum loss and distortion.

(3) Compliance-Gaining Competence: Competence associated with persuasion and securing an appropriate level of compliance and/or co-operation. (1989: 233)

The origins of this model in studies of business people working on projects in other countries are perhaps betrayed in the third competence particularly. What appears to be naive to FL teachers is the following statement:

> Certainly some knowledges are important to competence — at least some facets of competence as previously mentioned. Knowledge of language, for instance, is obviously important to cross-cultural information transfer. Is such knowledge — and perhaps knowledge of cultural and communication rules — not equally important to compliance-gaining and relationship-building? (1989: 234)

On the other hand, this kind of model reminds the FL teacher of the importance of seeing linguistic competence in a wider context. The model begins to expand and add detail to van Ek's notion of 'social competence' and 'sociocultural competence'.

The significance of linguistic competence is down-graded even further in the perspective taken by Gudykunst (1994), who argues that 'the processes operating when we communicate interculturally are the same as when we communicate intraculturally' (1994: x). It is not then surprising when he devotes only two pages to 'second-language competence'. His model of the 'competent communicator' focuses on psychological factors, and he makes the preliminary point that the judgement about competence in communication is one which is context-dependent and made by others in the context rather than in some absolute sense. His definition is therefore of 'perceived competence' and the components are as follows (Gudykunst, 1994: 159ff.):

Motivation: made up of a number of needs:

- for a sense of security as a human being;
- for a sense of predictability;
- for a sense of group inclusion;
- to avoid diffuse anxiety;
- for a sense of a common shared world;
- for symbolic/material gratification;
- to sustain our self-conceptions.

Knowledge: this includes cultural and linguistic knowledge but the implication is that foreign language competence is not essential: 'If we are familiar with or fluent in other people's language, for example, we can usually understand them better when they speak our language than if we know nothing about their language' (Gudykunst, 1994.: 169). Other kinds of knowledge are given more emphasis:

- knowledge of how to gather information;
- knowledge of personal similarities, as well as understanding differences;
- knowledge of alternative interpretation (this is not related to linguistic semantics but to interpretation of behaviour).

Skills: those skills in particular which are directly related to reducing uncertainty and anxiety:

- ability to be mindful, above all being 'cognitively aware' of the process of communication rather than the intended outcome;
- ability to tolerate ambiguity, to deal effectively with situations even when there is little objective information present and outcomes are difficult to predict;
- ability to manage anxiety;
- ability to empathise, involving cognitive, affective and communication components;
- ability to adapt, especially adapting behaviour to the expectations of others;
- ability to make accurate predictions and explanations of others' behaviour.

As suggested earlier, such a model is surprisingly lacking in reference to linguistic competence, mentioned only as a possible supportive factor. It could also be criticised for its categorisations of knowledge, skills and psychological factors. For example, 'how to gather information' might be better categorised as a skill, whereas 'ability to tolerate ambiguity' is a psychological trait rather than a skill, and is more related to issues of 'motivation'. The value of this model however lies less in the detail than in the perspective it suggests. Gudykunst is concerned to produce a practical guide to intergroup communication, one which will help in the management of the conflict 'inevitable in any relationship'. His approach reminds FL teachers that, since they have now become committed to FLT which prepares learners for face-to-face interaction with people of other (linguistic) groups, there are new psychological factors which have to be taken into account. FLT cannot confine its interest to the psychology of the learning or acquisition of linguistic and sociolinguistic competence, as it has hitherto.

One reaction to this situation is refusal to 'overload the boat', that is to accept responsibility for other than linguistic and sociolinguistic competence. This attitude is defended by referring to the limited amount of time available in most FLT courses, especially in the general education system. This is obviously an important issue. It can be resolved either by reducing the scope of the linguistic and sociolinguistic competences being pursued, or by extending the time and the nature of the activities in courses. For example, FL teachers are often responsible for 'visits and exchanges' and need to take account of the factors Gudykunst identifies in order to ensure that learners profit from and learn during visits and exchanges. They need to be aware of the Motivation, Knowledge and Skills involved and the learning theories which help them to plan the activities to ensure learning takes place (Whalley, 1997).

Communication and Interaction

One of the needs which Gudykunst includes in his characterisation of 'motivation' is 'the need for a sense of a common shared world'. The qualities of the 'competent communicator', which he identifies, are the psychological preconditions for satisfying this need, but a common shared world has to be *created* in interaction with other people. It is not simply there, waiting to be discovered and accessed.

One of the defining characteristics of a social group is the shared world which its members accept, and they in turn are accepted as members because they subscribe to the beliefs, behaviours and meanings of that shared world. This is however not a static condition. People become members of a group through a process of socialisation over time, and when they are members, they are constantly negotiating their common understanding of details, which over time may become major changes in their beliefs, behaviours or meanings. This much has been demonstrated in the work of symbolic interactionists (cf. O'Keefe & Delia, 1985).

A further dimension is added by the work of Bourdieu (1990) who argues that, within a society, power is differentially held by different social groups. They ensure that access to membership, to a 'field' of activity, is carefully controlled by requiring would-be members to have a specific cultural capital, which can be acquired only in particular educational institutions (Bourdieu, 1989). Christensen (1994) has taken Bourdieu's theory as the basis for considering how FLT should prepare learners for interaction with speakers of other languages. He writes from the particular perspective of Western Europe and its concern with political and social integration, an issue to which we shall return later, but his argument is that Bourdieu's concepts of 'field' and 'capital' should be used to describe what FLT should focus on. FLT should not introduce learners to a 'culture', to a particular combination of beliefs, behaviours and meanings dominant in a specific society, precisely because they are dominant and represent the interests of a powerful minority. Christensen is not explicit about how Bourdieu's concepts can be used in FLT but one can see that the aims might be expressed in terms of providing learners with the means of interacting with any speaker of another language, whatever field or capital they bring to the interaction, and on another occasion (1993) he argued that 'the quest for culture as essence and object has to be abandoned in favour of method, i.e. a process of investigation where every single social encounter potentially involves different values, opinions and world-views'. Thus learners are not limited to interaction only with those who have access to the dominant cultural capital. Instead their own cultural capital, even if not dominant in their own society, is valued in any interaction, as is the cultural capital of their interlocutors. This is particularly important for those learners who do not have access to the dominant culture in their own or another society and who are therefore not attracted by the worlds which FLT offers them. It is also important when the language is a lingua franca, and neither interlocutor is familiar with the cultural capital of the other.

Christensen's view makes very explicit the issue of power and access to power in society, as argued by Bourdieu, and its significance for FLT, and European integration. He argues with others (e.g. Becher, 1996) that European integration cannot take place for the individual — whatever the institutional changes — if they feel cut off from the fields and cultures promoted in schools, including in the FLT classroom. With respect to FLT, therefore, he argues against representation of a society's culture, because this inevitably means the choice of the culture which a dominant group has managed to make the 'national' culture of the society, even though it is accessible only to that group, not to the many other people in the society. Specifically, he argues against the adoption of Geertz's (1975: 89) definition of culture as 'an historically transmitted pattern of meanings embodied in symbols, a system of inherited conceptions expressed in a symbolic form by means of which men communicate, perpetuate and develop their knowledge about attitudes towards life' (see Byram, 1989a: 82). Apart from the fact that this 'pattern of meanings' is likely to be only that of the dominant group, this definition is too static, not allowing for the negotiation and change which go on within social groups and societies as a whole.

The implication of this interactionist perspective is that FLT should not attempt to provide representations of other cultures, but should concentrate on equipping learners with the means of accessing and analysing any cultural practices and meanings they encounter, whatever their status in a society. This would be a complete reversal of recent traditions in FLT where the provision of information about a country has been the major and sometimes only approach to equipping learners with sociocultural competence. The information has, moreover, been mainly about the institutions of a society and their history, complemented by an intuitive selection of representations of 'everyday life'. To replace this approach with one which focuses on processes and methods of analysing social processes and their outcomes, is to take seriously the issues of social power in FLT, to provide learners with critical tools and to develop their critical understanding of their own and other societies.

It may however be possible and desirable to combine these two approaches. First of all let us consider why learners need knowledge about the (dominant) culture of a society. Analysis of individuals' social identity defines this as that part of an individual's self-concept which derives from their knowledge of their membership of a social group (or groups) together with the value and emotional significance attached to that membership (Tajfel, 1978: 63; Vivian & Brown, 1995). The beliefs, behaviours and meanings which make up the practices of the group are what might be the 'content' or informational dimension of FLT, provided that a means is found to ensure that learners do not perceive these as 'objective' and fixed, but changing and negotiated over time by members of the group. Secondly, since individuals belong to many groups, the analysis of the social world to which they belong may in principle prioritise some groups over others. Bourdieu suggests that, in economically advanced societies, economic divisions are powerful and proposes that description of a society should be in those terms, but he also points out that:

> the fact remains that the strength of economic and social differences is never such that one cannot organise agents by means of other principles of division — ethnic, religious or national, for instance. (1990: 132)

It has been the tradition of FLT to analyse in terms of national divisions and national identity, tacitly accepting the fact that this is also above all the analysis of the culture of a dominant elite. Is this tradition justified?

The learner of a foreign language is likely to use the language in contact with people from another country, either a country where the language is spoken natively or a country whose language they do not speak. In the latter case, the foreign language serves as a lingua franca. In other situations, the learner meets people from their own country (for example anglophone Canadians learning French) but from a different ethnic group. In these three situations, the contact with someone from another group will reinforce their contrasting identities. As Tajfel says:

> The characteristics of one's group as a whole (...) achieve most of their significance in relation to perceived differences from other groups and the value connotations of these differences (...) the definition of a group (national or racial or any other) makes no sense unless there are other groups around. (1978: 66)

So, in the first two cases, the defining characteristics of the encounter will be those of national group identity, whereas in the third encounter, it will be intra-national ethnic differences which dominate.

The argument for developing learners' understanding of the beliefs, behaviours and meanings of the national group is then that it helps learners in inter-national communication and interaction. It is assumed that all interaction will make some reference to national identity and cultural beliefs and practices, even if the people involved are not part of the elite social group which has imposed them on the nation. A similar argument applies to the third case, of inter-ethnic communication. In the case of lingua franca, however, learners cannot acquire knowledge of all the national identities and cultures with which they may come into contact. In this case, the introduction to the national culture of a country where the language is spoken natively can serve as an example, but must be combined with developing in learners the methods to cope with other situations, based on this example. This supports the argument for a focus on methods, as well as content. It might also be support for an exclusive focus on methods, as we saw Christensen arguing earlier, but would this be justified?

The advantages, presented so far, of an emphasis on 'method', of providing learners with the means to analyse and thereby understand and relate to, whatever social world their interlocutors inhabit, are twofold. Method ensures that the representation of a society only in terms of the dominant elite culture is undermined; it is not the focus or perhaps even present at all in the course of study. Second, the emphasis on method prepares learners for encounters with cultural practices which have not been presented to them, and, in the case of lingua franca, cannot be anticipated. A third advantage is that through learning methods of analysis learners can also be encouraged to identify the ways in which particular cultural practices and beliefs maintain the social position and power of particular groups. The analysis can become critical. Furthermore, the analysis can be comparative, turning learners' attention back on their own practices, beliefs and social identities — and the groups to which they do or do not belong — and this analysis too can be critical (Byram, 1997a).

A fourth point will become relevant later when I propose a model of Intercultural Communicative Competence which is based on the concept of the 'intercultural speaker', but let it be raised here too in the discussion of power relationships in communication. There has long been an assumption in FLT that 'the native speaker is always right' (Kramsch, in press). Native speaker intuitions are called upon to resolve doubts about grammatical issues, idiomatic usage and even pronunciation, although the latter is a problematic area. Language learners aspire to the mastery of grammar and idiom of the educated native speaker using the standard language, and their accuracy is usually evaluated against that norm. Insofar as a minority of learners can attain the norm with respect to the grammar and linguistic competence, this approach seems acceptable. Even though it condemns the majority of learners to 'failure', it can be argued that convergence to the norm is needed to ensure efficient communication among foreign speakers of a language, just as a standard language is required for native speakers. There is no doubt, however, that in both cases those who master the norm — which in practice is the same standardised language — have a potential advantage over foreign speakers, and non-standard native speakers. When they take advantage of that potential, they exercise power over their interlocutors.

A similar situation may arise with respect to culture. The native speaker, especially if they are a member of the dominant group in a society, has the possibility of exercising power over the foreign speaker. The native speaker is 'always right', if both native and foreign speaker have an expectation in common that the learner shall acquire the culture(s) of a country where the language is spoken natively. The advantage of an FLT approach emphasising analysis of the interaction is that it allows learners to see their role not as imitators of native speakers but as social actors engaging with other social actors in a particular kind of communication and interaction which is different from that between native speakers. In this inter-national interaction, both interlocutors have a significant but different role, and the foreign speaker who knows something both of the foreign culture and of their own, is in a position of power at least equal to that of the native speaker. I shall return to this point in Chapter 2, in a closer definition of the 'intercultural speaker'.

The advantages of representing a national culture and cultural identity — the need to prepare learners for inter-national interactions — can therefore be combined with the advantages of a focus on critical and comparative method. The national culture will be seen as only one of the sets of cultural practices and beliefs to which an interlocutor subscribes — or is at least aware of as a framework for their actions and identity — and yet it provides learners with a basis for interaction. The learner has also acquired methods for transfer to other situations and the means of coping with new cultural practices and identities.

Finally, we must remember that FLT has a particular contribution to make to the preparation of learners for encounter with otherness, a contribution which complements that of other subject areas in the general education curriculum, notably human geography (McPartland *et al.*, 1996). FLT is centrally concerned with communication in a foreign *language*. The significance of this is not only the practical question of linguistic competence for communication, central though that is, but also the relationship between the language and cultural practices and beliefs of a group. Since language is a prime means of embodying the complexity of those practices and beliefs, through both reference and connotations (Byram, in press a), and the interplay of language and identity (Le Page & Tabouret-Keller, 1985), the acquisition of a foreign language is the acquisition of the cultural practices and beliefs it embodies for particular social groups, even though the learner may put it to other uses too. It is also the relativisation of what seems to the learner to be the natural language of their own identities, and the realisation that these are cultural, and socially constructed. Teaching for linguistic competence cannot be separated from teaching for intercultural competence.

Teaching Intercultural Communication in Context

In discussing whether there should be 'content' as well as 'method' in the cultural dimension of FLT, I gave three simple examples of intercultural communication:

- between people of different languages and countries where one is a native speaker of the language used;
- between people of different languages and countries where the language used is a lingua franca;
- and between people of the same country but different languages, one of whom is a native speaker of the language used.

This is a reminder that FLT always takes place in a particular context and that the nature of the Intercultural Communicative Competence required is partly dependent on context. Furthermore, if someone acquires ICC as a consequence of being taught in a formal sense, then they are part of a social institution which has its aims and purposes decided in part by external societal factors. We saw from the discussion of van Ek's model of communicative competence that he placed it firmly within a general educational framework, where the justification for FLT is partly in terms of its contribution to the personal development of the learner.

It is evident from this that before attempting a descriptive model of ICC, we need to consider to what extent contexts of communication and educational institutions might have an influence on the model. I shall discuss the case of FLT as part of general education, from primary through to lifelong, adult education. Some institutions may not claim to have general educational aims, such as those which train people for short placements in another country, but even these would not reject any educational development which takes place incidentally.

Let us consider some cases, starting with one where the function of the foreign language includes the concept of lingua franca. The Arab Gulf States have a general agreed approach to education, including FLT, to which each state subscribes. It may then formulate its own aims and purposes within the framework. The 'United Formula for Goals of Subjects in General Education Stages in the Arab Gulf States' includes the following foreign language objectives:

> At the end of the secondary stage students should:
> - acquire a favourable attitude to the English language;
> - acquire a good understanding of English speaking people on the condition that the above will *not* lead to the creation of a hostile or indifferent attitude to the students' Arab/Islamic culture.

Taking the specifications in more detail, in Qatar we find that they include aims which are orientated to communication with native speakers of English, for reasons of technological progress and as a means of understanding one's own as well as the culture of others:

> To acquire a basic communicative competence in order to be able to use English appropriately in real life situations, to appreciate the value of learning English as a means of communication with English speaking people, and to gain access to their knowledge in various fields and to the technology which has international currency.
>
> To expand one's own cultural awareness by learning about the cultural heritage of English speaking peoples and by so doing to arrive at a livelier appreciation of both cultures.

They also include lingua franca aims, both instrumental — to pursue studies — and liberal — to develop harmonious relationships:

> To provide the potential for pursuing academic studies or practical

> training in English speaking countries or in countries where English is, for some subjects, the medium of instruction.
>
> To increase by means of a common language the possibility of understanding, friendship and co-operation with all people who speak that language.

There is also an unusual and interesting particular aim for English as a lingua franca which may be a tacit purpose in many education systems but is here made explicit:

> To exploit one's command of English in order to spread in the world a better understanding and appreciation of one's own religion, culture, and values and to influence world public opinion favourably towards one's people and their causes. (Abu Jalalah, 1993: 22–23)

One might infer from the final statement that there is a need to change unfavourable opinions in the world. Events in the Gulf States in the early 1990s clearly created some unfavourable perceptions and, though these statements are all from an earlier date, they might be considered all the more pertinent. The kind of ICC required to fulfil these aims would involve learners acquiring an understanding of those unfavourable perceptions, and how to respond to them. The underlying theme is that FLT should provide opportunities for interaction with people from other countries but should not threaten or undermine the Arab and Islamic identity of learners themselves. A certain fear of 'Western' influences lies behind this, which may be justified by the increase in English-language television and other visual media (Al-Hail, 1995) and by a fear of 'linguistic imperialism' (Phillipson, 1992) although as Pennycook (1994) has shown, this view is easily over-simplified. Furthermore, as argued earlier with support form Tajfel, the encounter with otherness itself creates a clearer sense of one's own identity, an identity which some Arab governments wish to reinforce.

In a second case, Canada, the role of FLT with respect to the teaching of 'core French' is seen by some teachers as creating a better understanding of and potential for interaction with francophone Canadians (C. Leblanc *et al.*, 1990). Their recommendation is that learners' awareness of cultures and cultural identities should begin with their own but be gradually extended outwards, to the regional, provincial, national and international. However the main source of cultural understanding is '*la présence des francophones (in Canada), leur histoire (en ce qu'elle permet d'expliquer le présent), les parlers francophones, le quotidien des francophones et la dimension internationale de la francophonie*' (R. Leblanc, 1990: 10). Although there is no explicit statement about attitudes towards francophone Canadians, it is evident in recommendations for pedagogy that there is an intention to create more harmonious relationships:

> *A un niveau avancé une prise de conscience des préjugés dominants peut être bénéfique. Il s'agira avant tout de mettre en valeur le caractère exagéré des stéréotypes, non de forcer des attitudes positives à l'égard des francophones. Il ne faut pas sous-estimer les jeunes en évitant ou en sur-simplifiant un sujet difficile.* (C. Leblanc *et al.*, 1990: 39)

As in the case of the Arab Gulf States, the political context, this time within the state, is clearly influencing the aims and methods of FLT. The increased support for Quebec separatism in the mid-1990s made the concerns of these authors, representatives of the '*Association canadienne des professeurs de langues secondes*', all the more relevant.

A third example is the European situation. The increasing integration and co-operation between European states is a consequence of political union in the West and the opening of political frontiers in the East and Centre. Two political organisations reflect and influence these changes, and have introduced a 'European' perspective into education and FLT. The Council of Europe has related these changes directly to FLT through a programme of research and development with the title 'Language Learning for European Citizenship'. In this context, 'European Citizenship' was susceptible of an interpretation referring to closer political unification and also, more loosely, as 'citizenship in Europe', without necessarily implying closer political unity. The intention was to emphasise 'the strengthening of the individual's independence of thought and action combined with social responsibility as a citizen in a participatory pluralist democratic society'. This would combine 'autonomy with the idea of an emerging European identity and political convergence' (Trim, 1996) As well as encouraging development in specific areas of FLT — such as FLT in the primary school or in upper secondary — the programme focuses upon ways to facilitate mobility between states; the Council of Europe includes both East and West. One purpose was to produce a 'Common European Framework for Language Teaching and Learning' which will enable all involved — teachers, learners, examiners, curriculum designers — to define their work and relate it to a commonly recognised description of aims and objectives and levels of assessment for different aspects of communicative competence. If successful this will influence national definitions of aims, objectives and assessment, and the underlying interpretation of 'communicative competence'.

The European Union has a more limited membership and comprises Western European countries only, although Eastern European countries hope to join and its influence is therefore wider than its current membership. The European Community, as it then was, also introduced a programme for education to encourage a 'European Dimension' in schools, universities and other institutions. Here, too, the concept of mobility across frontiers is fundamental and is formulated in terms of economic and social advantages:

> (the measures introduced should help to) make young people aware of the advantages which the Community represents, but also of the challenges it involves, in opening up an enlarged economic and social area to them. (*Bulletin of the European Communities*, 5 (1988): 10)

There is also an explicit reference to 'European identity', which is not defined precisely but associated with knowledge about European civilisation:

> (the measures introduced should help to) strengthen in young people a sense of European identity and make clear to them the value of European civilisation and of the foundations on which the European peoples intend to base their development today, that is in particular the safe-guarding of the principles of democracy, social justice and respect for human rights. (*Bulletin of the European Communities*, 5 (1988): 10)

The scope of the European Dimension is to include 'all appropriate disciplines, for example, literature, languages, history, geography, social sciences, economics and the arts' (*Bulletin of the European Communities*, 5 (1988): 11).

The effect on FLT varies from one member state to another. In Britain, the curriculum for England and Wales reflects European Union membership in that schools must offer an official EU language as a foreign language and they may offer, in addition, a non-EU language if demand and resources permit; they may not offer a non-EU language as the only foreign language. This is a tangible policy consequence. Other consequences are less easily traced directly to the European Dimension, since the dominant foreign languages have always been French, German and Spanish. Nonetheless, in a report written in preparation for the introduction of the national curriculum, there are several references to the significance of membership of the European Community/Union, including specific discussion of the document cited above:

> European awareness is thus one aspect of international awareness and fits well with one of the main aims of modern language learning, namely, the development in learners of sensitivity to the culture (in its

> widest sense) of the communities whose languages are being studied. (DES, 1990: 49)

The report goes on to emphasise that it places 'a high value on cultural awareness', and suggests a number of approaches and methods to put this into operation, including collaboration with teachers of other subjects. It concludes by saying:

> In these and other ways learners can come to identify with the experience and perspectives of people in the countries and communities where the language is spoken. This should both contribute to meeting the requirements and objectives of the European Community Resolution on the European Dimension and place these within the broader international context. (DES, 1990: 49)

It is therefore clear that European policy has a direct effect on national policy and, as a consequence of the specific recommendations for practice, works through to the school classroom. The kind of cultural awareness which FLT is expected to develop in learners is defined in terms deriving from the socio-political context. In a more recent development, the European Commission (1996) has suggested in a White Paper, that all European citizens should speak three languages. This could imply two compulsory foreign languages in British school curricula rather than one at present. It remains to be seen whether this political demand will be followed too.

A fourth case is the United States, where language learning is not obligatory during compulsory schooling, and where many learners have an obligatory course during the first phase of their higher education. This is not to say that schools do not have a significant role in FLT, and there are a wide range of languages taught, and a variety of approaches to the teaching and learning process. There are immersion courses for anglophone pupils of primary school age in European and East Asian languages. There are dual language programmes in which anglophone pupils are taught together with children who already have some competence in the language in question because of their home background. There are 'less commonly taught' languages such as Arabic, Chinese, Hebrew, Japanese, Portuguese and Russian, as well as the dominant European languages, French German and Spanish. The aims vary in part as a function of the language for the individual and society. Many children study a language because it has 'heritage' significance for them and their parents. The role of Spanish in the United States, where estimates suggest that there will be more speakers of Spanish than of English by the first decades of the next century, means that the aims and purposes are quite different from those for French and

German. In a document setting 'National Standards' for language learning in schools, the variety of aims and purposes is acknowledged and an enriched definition of goals for language learning is proposed:

> Regardless of the reason for study, foreign languages have something to offer to everyone. It is with this philosophy in mind that the standards task force identified five goal areas that encompass all these reasons: Communication, Cultures, Connections, Comparisons, and Communities — five C's of foreign language education.
>
> *Communication*, or communicating in languages other than English, is at the heart of second language study, whether the communication takes place face-to-face, in writing, or across centuries through the reading of literature. Through the study of other languages, students gain a knowledge and understanding of the *cultures* that use that language; in fact, students cannot truly master the language until they have also mastered the cultural contexts in which the language occurs. Learning languages provides *connections* to additional bodies of knowledge that are unavailable to monolingual English speakers. Through *comparisons* and contrasts with the language being studied, students develop greater insight into their own language and culture and realise that multiple ways of viewing the world exist. Together, these elements enable the student of languages to participate in multilingual *communities* at home and around the world in a variety of contexts and in culturally appropriate ways. (*Standards for Foreign Language Learning*, 1996: 23)

It is significant however that the authors feel they have to anticipate the argument that many Americans will not need a foreign language after school either because of the strength of English as a world language or because they are unlikely to travel outside the United States. They argue from the significance of cultural learning and the acquisition of intercultural competence:

> Even if students never speak the language after leaving school, for a lifetime they will retain the crosscultural skills and knowledge, the insight, and the access to a world beyond traditional borders. (*Standards for Foreign Language Learning*, 1996: 24)

In these circumstances, it is particularly important that learning focused on a language which may never be used outside school — such as German or Russian — should give a high priority to the acquisition of skills, attitudes and knowledge which are transferable to situations both within and beyond national frontiers where cultural awareness and sensitivity is required. The acquisition of another language, or even part of one, may be less important and less feasible in the time available than the application of such transferable competences, including the knowledge of how to manage communication in intercultural interactions (Brecht & Walton, 1995).

Assessment in Context of Intercultural Communicative Competence

We have seen that the formulation of objectives for FLT is influenced by contextual factors. Clearly formulated objectives are essential to proper assessment, and assessment itself is therefore indirectly affected by contextual factors. If, for example, the Gulf States objective of being able to influence world opinion with respect to one's own culture is taken seriously, then assessment should include some kind of measure of learners' ability to do this.

Social factors affect assessment more directly too. FLT as part of general education usually takes place in an institution which has the responsibility of guaranteeing the abilities of their graduates. There are therefore very careful processes involved in certification. In some societies more than others, certification is crucial to the individual's future; it has the function of a *laissez-passer* through the narrow gates of access to further education, promotion and success. Where large numbers of people wish to use their certificates outside the country of issue, the question of mutual recognition becomes crucial. This is increasingly the case in Europe, and the aim of the Council of Europe's 'Common European Framework for Language Learning and Teaching', mentioned above, is to facilitate mutual recognition.

Because certification and its guarantees are crucial to learners and their employers or educators, they have to be open to scrutiny and susceptible of reasoned justification, all the more so where mutual recognition is sought. One approach to this is to concentrate only on those aspects of ICC which can be clearly designated and measured. Yet this does not take account of our increasing recognition of the complexity of communication and interaction across cultural and linguistic borders. There is a risk of over-simplifying and misrepresenting a learner's ability in order to ensure objectivity in measurement. The social pressure for clarity in certification cannot however be ignored and has to be taken into account in the assessment of the those aspects of ICC which have only recently been recognised and not yet fully described and defined for assessment purposes.

Problems of certification within educational institutions are compounded if learners' competence acquired in other circumstances is also to be recognised and certificated. There are practical difficulties which arise from not being able to use techniques of continuous assessment within the teaching process. It can also be argued that competence acquired outside institutional settings and without the guidance of a teacher, will not necessarily have involved general educational processes and experiences. Should there be certification, and therefore assessment, of a level of general education, of a capacity for insight, of an acquisition of certain humane values and morals, of a potential to act in accordance with these?

We have seen in this chapter that the definition of ICC is a complex matter. There are different theoretical emphases which can determine our understanding of what is involved and how widely the concept should be defined. Should we emphasise knowledge of cultures and cultural practices or rather the capacity and skills of conscious analysis of intercultural interaction? Should we include non-verbal communication? Should we pay attention to psychological traits or focus only on capacity to act? We have also seen that definitions are in practice influenced by social and political factors, by the fact that FLT often takes place within institutions of general education subject to the requirements of society. When we consider assessment, similar social factors have also to be taken into account: assessment is not simply a technical matter for it is often associated with certification and increasingly with recognition across political frontiers.

Our task in the next chapter is thus not an easy one: to offer a definition and description of ICC which is general enough to be of significance but nonetheless takes into account the issues raised in this chapter.

Notes

1. I do not intend to include here a comprehensive review of the literature. This has been done on a number of occasions: Byram, 1989; Knapp & Knapp-Potthoff, 1990; Dirven & Putz, 1993; Jaeger, 1995.
2. Habermas's work was much less influential in language teaching dominated by English as a Foreign Language, perhaps because of the level of abstraction and the language barrier. It is however particularly well used as a basis for discussing sociocultural competence by Melde (1987) discussed in detail in Byram, Morgan *et al.* (1994).
3. This work was part of the internal development papers for the Council of Europe's proposed Common European Framework.
4. I shall use this rather awkward phrase instead of reviewing the literature on defining culture, or attempting to produce my own water-tight definition. The phrase is a description of those aspects of culture, however defined, which are important for my purposes and which will become evident throughout the text. I shall discuss the issues in more detail in Chapter 2.
5. Poyatos (1993) gives a wide-ranging and thorough account of this 'triple structure of communication' and other paralinguistic phenomena, including examples from different cultures, but does not develop further his proposals for a syllabus.

Chapter 2

A Model for Intercultural Communicative Competence

Introduction

We saw in Chapter 1 that descriptions of intercultural communication must take into consideration the social context in which it takes place. They must also take account of the non-verbal dimensions of communication, and the limitations of descriptions which focus on language learning as traditionally conceived. I argued that, although the complexities should not be forgotten, the model which might be proposed needs to be accessible to and useful for teachers of foreign languages working within particular traditions and conceptualisations of their role as instructors and educators. This is not to say that a model cannot break out of the existing traditions, but it must be linked to them and usable within the constraints of current and foreseeable circumstances. Furthermore, we must also bear in mind that the model should be helpful for both teaching and assessment, and that assessment has a number of purposes, including certification.

In this chapter, I propose to describe in more detail the factors involved in intercultural communication and then consider how these factors are related to the competences which FL teachers traditionally attempt to develop in their learners. I shall for this purpose return to the models of communicative competence discussed in Chapter 1. In a third stage, I shall attempt to categorise the socio-cultural factors not usually taken into consideration by FL teachers, with a view to considering how they can be integrated into existing practices. The purpose of this chapter is therefore to propose a model of ICC which is as comprehensive as possible. The model will not be appropriate for all situations, since FLT varies from one situation to another as we saw earlier; it will remain a 'content-free' model until I suggest ways in which it can be used for specific situations in a later chapter.

Describing Intercultural Communication and the 'Intercultural Speaker'

Whatever a person's linguistic competence in a foreign language, when they interact socially with someone from a different country.[1] they bring to the situation their knowledge of the world which includes in some cases a substantial knowledge of the country in question and in others a minimal knowledge, of its geographical position or its current political climate, for example. Diplomats and foreign correspondents, or visiting teachers and exchange students, can be provided with information from official sources and can often find published guides. Their knowledge also includes their own country, although this may be less conscious, and they may not be aware of its significance in the interaction.

Their knowledge of their own country is a part of the social identity which they bring to the situation, and which is crucial for their interlocutor. For it is important to remember that the interaction between two individuals can only be fully understood when the relationship of the 'host' to the 'visitor' is included. The mutual perceptions of the social identities of the interlocutors is a determining factor in the interaction. They may share some knowledge of each other's country and they may share one or more of their social identities — their professional identity, for example in the case of diplomats or FL teachers — or they may be almost completely unknown to each other, as in the first visits of groups from one town to its twin town.

It will be evident from this that we cannot describe such an interaction as if there were two 'native-speakers' of the language involved, one of whom is a true native and the other attempting to be so. Yet, as suggested in Chapter 1, this is often the assumption when only the linguistic competence of each is in question: there is the native and there is a learner attempting to reach native or 'near-native' competence. Even this image has been criticised in recent times because the concept of native speaker linguistic competence is imprecise and unusable (Kramsch, in press), and it is more appropriate to develop an intercultural style, and tact, to overcome divergence rather than accept the norm of the monolingual (Kasper, 1995). Consideration of the interlocutors as social actors with social identities renders the image even more unusable. It is clear that, in a dyadic interaction for example, both interlocutors have different social identities and therefore a different kind of interaction than they would have with someone from their own country speaking the same language. It is for this reason that I shall introduce the concept of the 'intercultural speaker' to describe interlocutors involved in intercultural communication and interaction.

The success of such interaction can be judged in terms of the effective exchange of information, as has been the tendency in much communicative language teaching, but also in terms of the establishing and maintenance of human relationships. The latter in particular depends on attitudinal factors, for example the willingness of the interlocutors to expect problems of communication caused by lack of overlap in their respective knowledge of the world and of each other's country. It may depend on the ability of the interlocutors to accept criticism of the values they share with people in their usual social groups, and of which they may not have been consciously aware. It may also depend on their willingness to accept at least initially that they will be perceived by their interlocutor as a representative of a particular country, its values and its political actions, whatever their own views of these.

Knowledge and attitude factors are preconditions, although I shall argue that they are also modified by the processes of intercultural communication. The nature of the processes is a function of the skills which a person brings to the interaction. These can be divided into two broad and related categories: first, skills of interpretation and establishing relationships between aspects of the two cultures; second, skills of discovery and interaction. The former involve the ability to analyse data from one's own and from another country and the potential relationships between them. Skills of discovery can be operated in some circumstances independently of, and in others in combination with, skills of interaction. New data may be discovered in interaction with interlocutors from another country in particular times and places, and new data may also be gathered from other documents and sources without the need for interaction. Whatever their provenance, these data need to be part of the analysis of relationships.

These four aspects of interaction across frontiers of different countries — knowledge, attitudes, skills of interpreting and relating, and skills of discovery and interaction — can in principle be acquired through experience and reflection, without the intervention of teachers and educational institutions. If they are acquired with the help of a teacher, there is an option for the teacher to embed the learning process within a broader educational philosophy. For example, the teacher may wish to promote learner autonomy and create modes of teaching and learning accordingly (Holec, 1980; Nunan, 1988). I shall argue for the integration of teaching for intercultural communication within a philosophy of political education[2] (Doyé, 1993; Melde, 1987), and the development of learners' critical cultural awareness, with respect to their own country and others (Byram, 1997).

Based on these preliminary reflections, I propose a schema of the factors involved and the relationships among them, which I shall then discuss in more detail (see Figure 2.1).

	Skills interpret and relate (*savoir comprendre*)	
Knowledge of self and other; of interaction: individual and societal (*savoirs*)	**Education** political education critical cultural awareness (*savoir s'engager*)	**Attitudes** relativising self valuing other (*savoir être*)
	Skills discover and/or interact (*savoir apprendre/faire*)	

Figure 2.1 Factors in intercultural communication[3]

Attitudes

We are concerned here only with attitudes towards people who are perceived as different in respect of the cultural meanings, beliefs and behaviours they exhibit, which are implicit in their interaction with interlocutors from their own social group or others. Such attitudes are frequently characterised as prejudice or stereotype (Allport, 1979), and are often but not always negative, creating unsuccessful interaction. Attitudes which are the pre-condition for successful intercultural interaction need to be not simply positive, since even positive prejudice can hinder mutual understanding. They need to be attitudes of curiosity and openness, of readiness to suspend disbelief and judgement with respect to others' meanings, beliefs and behaviours. There also needs to be a willingness to suspend belief in one's own meanings and behaviours, and to analyse them from the viewpoint of the others with whom one is engaging. This is an ability to 'decentre' which Kohlberg *et al.* (1983) have argued is an advanced stage of psychological development and which Melde (1987) suggests is fundamental to understanding other cultures (cf. Byram *et al.*, 1994: 20–24). In an extreme case it can lead to a 're-socialisation', which Berger and Luckmann call 'alternation' (1966: 176), where individuals dismantle their preceding structure of subjective reality and re-construct it according to new norms. It involves a challenge to the norms of primary socialisation and, with respect to foreign language learning, learners may undergo a process of what I have called 'tertiary socialisation' (Byram, 1989b; Doyé, 1992).

The relationship of the attitudes factor with others is one of interdependence. Without relativising one's own and valuing others' experience, interpreting and relating them is likely to be value-laden. Although entirely value-free interpretation and relating are unlikely, nonetheless the raising of awareness about one's own values allows a conscious control of biased interpretation. The relationship between attitudes and knowledge is not the simple cause and effect often assumed, i.e. that increased knowledge creates positive attitudes (Byram, Morgan *et al.*, 1994). Nonetheless, it is probably easier to relativise one's own meanings, beliefs and behaviours through comparison with others' than to attempt to decentre and distance oneself from what the processes of socialisation have suggested is natural and unchangeable. Thirdly, the skills of discovery and interaction are less difficult to operate, less likely to involve psychological stress (Furnham & Bochner, 1986; Kim, 1988) if the person involved has attitudes of openness and curiosity. Finally, in an educational framework which aims to develop *critical* cultural awareness, relativisation of one's own and valuing of others' meanings, beliefs and behaviours does not happen without a reflective and analytical challenge to the ways in which they have been formed and the complex of social forces within which they are experienced.

Knowledge

The knowledge individuals bring to an interaction with someone from another country can be described in two broad categories: knowledge about social groups and their cultures in one's own country, and similar knowledge of the interlocutor's country on the one hand; knowledge of the processes of interaction at individual and societal levels, on the other hand. The first category is knowledge which may be more or less refined, but always present in some degree, whereas the second, involving knowledge about concepts and processes in interaction, is fundamental to successful interaction but not acquired automatically.

With respect to the first category, the inevitability of some knowledge being present is due to the processes of socialisation. Through primary socialisation largely in the family and secondary socialisation usually in formal education, the individual acquires knowledge, some remaining conscious, some unconscious and taken for granted, of the social groups to which they gain membership, and of other social groups with which they have contact. In countries with formal education systems, the knowledge acquired is often dominated by the notion of a 'national' culture and identity, and individuals acquire in varying degrees a national identity through socialisation in formal education. They also acquire other identities, regional, ethnic, social class and so on, through formal and informal socialisation. The knowledge they have of the shared beliefs, meanings and behaviours of these different groups includes a conscious awareness of two kinds of characteristic: those which are emblematic for the group — for example items of dress or modes of greeting; and those which it uses to differentiate itself from other groups, and mark its boundaries (Barth, 1969). The latter often include stories from its history, its institutions, its religious values, and are highly conscious, whereas other characteristics are usually taken for granted and only raised to consciousness when there is a need for contrast with other groups. They can be all the more influential in contact with other groups because they are unconscious and unanalysed.

Knowledge about other countries and the identities brought to an interaction by an interlocutor from another country, is usually 'relational', i.e. it is knowledge acquired within socialisation in one's own social groups and often presented in contrast to the significant characteristics of one's national group and identity. For example, knowledge of the history of another country is through the stories from the history of one's own nation-state, and is consequently a different interpretation to the story told within the foreign country. Often the stories told are prejudiced and stereotyped, particularly in processes of informal socialisation, within the family or in the media, for example. It follows that the greater the proximity and the more contacts there are and have been between the individual's country and that of their interlocutor, the more knowledge of each other there will be present in the interaction. Of course in the contemporary world, proximity is not only a matter of geographical distance, easily overcome by modern communications networks, but is rather a question of dominance in media and politics. Knowledge of the United States is probably universal, though differing according to the individual's country of origin and the power relationships between one's country and the USA, whereas knowledge of a country such as Denmark differs considerably from one part of the world to another.

The relational nature of the knowledge of other countries, and the beliefs, meanings and behaviours imputed to an interlocutor, are linked to the second category of knowledge in an interaction: knowledge of the *processes* of interaction at individual and societal level. If an individual knows about the ways in which their social identities have been acquired, how they are a prism through which other members of their group are perceived, and how they in turn perceive their interlocutors from another group, that awareness provides a basis for successful interaction. This declarative knowledge though necessary is not sufficient, and needs to be complemented by procedural knowledge of how to act in specific circumstances. In this sense, it is linked with the skills of interpreting and relating, of using existing knowledge to understand a specific document or behaviour for example, and to relate these to comparable but different documents or behaviours in their own social group. At one level, it is well-known that tea-drinking has different significance in different cultures; at another level a policy document on 'the centralisation of education' might be 'conservative' in one context and 'progressive' in another. The significance of behaviour or document cannot be taken for granted. Similarly, the skills of discovery and interaction are the means of augmenting and refining knowledge about the other and knowing how to respond to specific features of interaction with a particular individual.

Skills

An individual coming across a 'document', used in the widest sense, from another country can interpret it with the help of specific information and general frames of knowledge which will allow them to discover the allusions and connotations present in the document. The knowledge may have been acquired through formal education or by other, informal, means, but is likely to be conscious knowledge, consciously applied. Interpretation of a document from one's own environment is usually dependent on both conscious and taken-for-granted knowledge and the latter in particular may obscure from the individual the ethnocentric values and connotations in the document which would make it difficult to access for someone from another country.

The ability to interpret a document from one country for someone from another, or to identify relationships between documents from different countries, is therefore dependent on knowledge of one's own and the other environment. Moreover, in establishing relationships, the individual will discover both common ground, easily translated concepts and connotations, and lacunae (Ertelt-Vieth, 1991) or dysfunctions, including mutually contradictory meanings. The interpretation of one document in relationship to another or the translation of a document to make it accessible to someone from another country, necessarily includes handling dysfunctions and contradictions in order to resolve them where possible, but also in order to identify unresolvable issues.

This skill of interpreting and relating draws upon existing knowledge. The issue of how much and which kind of knowledge might be acquired through formal education, notably in the foreign language classroom, is one to which we shall return. Furthermore this skill can be distinguished from the skills of discovery and interaction in that it need not involve interaction with an interlocutor, but may be confined to work on documents. As a consequence, the individual is able to determine their own timescale for interpretation, not constrained by the demands of social interaction.

The skill of discovery may also be operated in the individual's own time, but equally it may be part of social interaction. The skill of discovery comes into play where the individual has no, or only a partial existing knowledge framework. It is the skill of building up specific knowledge as well as an understanding of the beliefs, meanings and behaviours which are inherent in particular phenomena, whether documents or interactions. The knowledge acquired may be 'instrumental' or 'interpretative'. The latter may operate without direct contact with people of another country but nonetheless satisfy curiosity and openness, as in the case argued for the United States where learners may never use the foreign language in interaction but nonetheless need to relate to other countries and cultures. In the former case, the individual might be geographically mobile and need to discover the ways to gain access to a new society, the institutions giving permissions for travel and residence, the institutions which manage relations between the host country and the country of origin. The skill of discovery is the ability to recognise significant phenomena in a foreign environment and to elicit their meanings and connotations, and their relationship to other phenomena. Although the skill is essentially identical in different environments, it may be more difficult to operate in those which have least in common with the individual's country of origin, the so-called 'exotic' languages and cultures. However, given the power of international media and popular culture, it is likely that the individual will be able to identify some phenomena in the most distant environments, although it cannot be assumed that they have the same meaning and significance.

One mode of discovery is obviously through social interaction, even though this adds constraints of time and mutual perceptions and attitudes mentioned earlier. The skill of interaction is above all the ability to manage these constraints in particular circumstances with specific interlocutors.[4] The individual needs to draw upon their existing knowledge, have attitudes which sustain sensitivity to others with sometimes radically different origins and identities, and operate the skills of discovery and interpretation. In particular, the individual needs to manage dysfunctions which arise in the course of interaction, drawing upon knowledge and skills. They may also be called upon not only to establish a relationship between their own social identities and those of their interlocutor, but also to act as mediator between people of different origins and identities. It is this function of establishing relationships, managing dysfunctions and mediating which distinguishes an 'intercultural speaker', and makes them different from a native speaker.

Intercultural Communication in Operation

The intention in this chapter so far has been to discuss intercultural communication at a generalisable level of abstraction. I have largely avoided illustrations, though these often help to clarify an argument. I have even avoided, as far as possible, reference to a 'culture', preferring instead the phrase 'beliefs, meanings and behaviours', in order not to commit the description to a particular definition of 'culture'. On the other hand I have referred to interaction between people of different countries, and it can be argued that this implies an unnecessary distinction between inter-country (or inter-cultural) and intra-country (or intra-cultural) interaction. We need therefore to develop the argument by asking whether there are limitations and conditions to be imposed on the general description given so far.

Definitions of 'culture' are many and rather than add to the attempts to produce a definitive and all-purpose definition, I want to suggest that we need a definition to suit the purposes of the foreign language teacher. This can begin, as I suggested on an earlier occasion (Byram, 1989a: 81ff.), with the beliefs and knowledge which members of a social group share by virtue of their membership. To describe these as 'shared meanings' is to open a link to language, in which they are embodied and to a view of language learning as learning the meanings of a specific social group. As indicated in Chapter 1, this view can be criticised as too static, not taking into account the constant negotiation and production of meanings in any interaction (Street, 1993). It can also be argued that it leads to emphasis on the meanings shared by a politically dominant elite group within a society. Furthermore, it was suggested in Chapter 1 that an account of interaction and communication should include non-verbal behaviour, and this has tacitly been acknowledged in the phrase 'beliefs, meanings and behaviours'. There is also an argument for including behaviour which is not directly related to communication and interaction, such as conventions and taboos of clothing, since the task of the FL teacher is to equip learners with the knowledge, attitudes and skills for relating to whatever experience they might have during a period of residence in another country or in interaction with someone from another country in their own society. As with other dimensions, the decision on how inclusive the treatment of non-verbal behaviour depends on the purposes of FLT. Where preparation for mobility and a period of residence and face-to-face interaction is insignificant, it can be argued that there is little point in including the non-verbal.

We have to be aware of the dangers of presenting 'a culture' as if it were unchanging over time or as if there were only one set of beliefs, meanings and behaviours in any given country. When individuals interact, they bring to the situation their own identities and cultures and if they are not members of a dominant group, subscribing to the dominant culture, their interlocutor's knowledge of that culture will be dysfunctional. In his argument against the representation of the culture of a particular country by its dominant beliefs, meanings and behaviours, Christensen (1994) suggests, as we saw in Chapter 1, that we should not think in terms of encounters between different language and culture systems, but rather of encounters between individuals with their own meanings and cultural capital:

> It is not a question of different culture and language systems which confront each other in cultural encounters, but of interacting individuals who produce, negotiate or defend meanings and capitals. Seen in this way there is in theory no *absolute* difference between encounters between individuals from different countries and within the same country. (1994: 37 — my translation, author's emphasis)

He goes on to argue that although there may be a link between geographical and social proximity, with a consequent sharing of meanings, the link is not a necessary one. People who are geographically separated may share meanings, and FL teachers often refer to and make use of shared youth cultures. Christensen therefore concludes that:

> The assumption that cultural encounter can be understood as an encounter between two individuals, each with their origins in different socio-geographical spaces (country = culture) cannot be used in analysis. (1994: 38)

This is a useful reminder and an important emphasis on the individuality of interaction. It raises the question of whether there is, in principle, any difference between 'intercultural' and 'intracultural' communicative competence, in the sense of communication within and across national or state frontiers, between people of the same or different national speech communities, i.e. where both or only one — or indeed neither — are native speakers. I have implied earlier in this chapter, by referring to different *countries*, that there is a worthwhile analytical distinction, which becomes clear if we complement Christensen's use of Bourdieu's sociological framework with social psychological and linguistic perspectives.

From the social psychological perspective, we are reminded that in a social encounter, the participants attribute characteristics and identities to each other, (Tajfel, 1981). In an encounter between people from different countries, one of the initial attributions is usually, though not always, that of national identity. This is particularly the case if there are indications, by accent for example, of the interlocutor's native language, even though this may be misleading and influence the interlocutor to impute the wrong identity. In these situations the attribution is to a socio-geographical entity, a country, and to the dominant culture within that culture insofar as it is known. Christensen's point would be of course that this creates the wrong starting point and introduces issues of power and dominance which we should strive to avoid by giving learners the skills to analyse the dominant representations and their origins, a point with which I would agree, as indicated earlier in this chapter. The social psychological perspective also reminds us however that attributions other than nationality occur simultaneously: gender, ethnicity, age, social class and others. Where one of these is more important to the individuals or is given dominance by the particular context of the interaction, national identity and presumed culture will not be an issue, or will soon be ignored. Language difference is minimised, although a linguistic perspective suggests that it cannot be forgotten, which Christensen appears to do.

The language learning perspective suggests that the subjective experience of interaction in a foreign language distinguishes significantly between inter-cultural/country and intra-cultural/country communication. The FL speaker may experience a degree of powerlessness *vis à vis* a native speaker.[5] They may sense the constraints of insufficient knowledge and skill in linguistic competence to meet the specific requirements of the interaction. They should also be aware of the need to compare, contrast and establish relationships between concepts in their own and the foreign language, including the problems of dysfunction and conflict.

I conclude therefore that though sociologically speaking there is no difference in principle between inter- and intra-cultural communication, for the FL teacher the psychological analysis suggests that the difference is significant. The skills, attitudes and knowledge described earlier in this chapter are clearly related to those involved in intra-cultural communication, but are sufficiently different to warrant specific attention. The FL learner needs a particular kind of socio-cultural competence in addition to what they may have already acquired in their own country and language community.

This raises a further question: whether a native speaker participant in an intercultural interaction needs a competence different to that operating in interaction with other native speakers from their own society. In societies where there is considerable mobility, an individual's experience of otherness of language and culture may be just as frequently in the role of 'host' or recipient, as in the role of traveller and 'guest'. This has been the case for many Western Europeans for the last three or four decades. The success of interaction being dependent on both interlocutors, the notion of intercultural communicative competence can be used to describe the capacities of a host as much as a guest. Although the host will often speak in their native language they need the same kinds of knowledge, attitudes and skills as their guest to understand and maintain relationships between meanings in the two cultures. They need the ability to decentre and take up the other's perspective on their own culture, anticipating and where possible resolving dysfunctions in communication and behaviour. They may have specific knowledge of the other's culture or only a general awareness of the issues involved in intercultural communication. The former would be the case if they have learnt something of the other's language and culture, in the FL classroom for example, and this suggests that FLT should explicitly include the host role in its aims and methods. It does not require additional skills or knowledge, but rather the development of the individual's awareness of the differences in the roles of 'host' or 'guest', and in particular, awareness of the power of the interlocutor using their native language, and the means by which that power can be shared with non-native interlocutors.

A final operational question is that of degrees of competence and performance. This anticipates our later discussion of the process of assessment and here I shall only raise the issues in principle. One fundamental question is whether there is a 'threshold' below which an individual cannot be deemed to have intercultural communicative competence at all. A second question is whether there are degrees of competence beyond the threshold, and if so whether they are measurable. Some previous work in Europe (e.g. Campos *et al.* 1988; Meyer, 1991) focuses upon the description of levels of competence leading to intercultural competence, and implies that there is a threshold below which individuals cannot be deemed to operate successfully. The discussions do not address the question of whether it is meaningful to seek to describe levels beyond the threshold, or whether they can be measured. Other work, in the United States, suggests four levels of competence (Singerman, 1996) but gives less emphasis to the concept of interculturality and mediation. Moreover, it too describes levels below a threshold, its fourth level being closest to our description of the knowledge, attitudes and skills required:

> Upon reaching each of the stages below, the learner (...):
> **Stage 4**
> - recognises the importance of understanding manifestations of the target culture in terms of its own context;
> - is aware of his/her own cultural perspective and of how this perspective influences one's perception of phenomena;
> - can act and react in a culturally appropriate way while being aware of his/her 'otherness'.
>
> (Singerman, 1996: 12)

It is implied that once this stage is reached, there is no further gradation of competence required.

Given the significance of contexts in determining aims, discussed in Chapter 1, it is clear that the ability to describe and certificate levels of competence below a threshold of intercultural competence is useful. Where the circumstances demand intercultural competence as a *sine qua non* of success — as is arguably the case in full mobility for work and residence in another country — then the question of whether and how levels can be identified beyond the threshold becomes particularly significant. This is an issue to which we shall return.

Acquiring Intercultural Communicative Competence in an Educational Setting

Much acquisition of Intercultural Communicative Competence is tutored and takes place within an educational setting. Some educational institutions may fulfil functions other than those of general education and focus on vocational skills or short-term objectives. Otherwise, institutions and teachers, including FL teachers, have a responsibility to pursue general educational aims together with those of the subject taught. In the model proposed here, I want to focus on political education as a part of general education because it has a particular relationship with ICC.

Doyé (1993) draws parallels between foreign language education and '*politische Bildung*' as understood in the German tradition of schooling. He bases his analysis on Gagel's (1983) distinction of three kinds of 'orientation' to be offered across all subjects to young people during their general education:

- cognitive orientation: the acquisition of concepts, knowledge and modes of analysis for the understanding of political phenomena;
- evaluative orientation: the explanation and mediation of values and the ability to make political judgements on the basis of these values;
- action orientation: development of the ability and the readiness for political engagement.

In the FL classroom, Doyé argues, there is congruence between these dimensions of political education and the aims and methods of FLT:

- cognitive orientation: the international dimension of the acquisition of knowledge about and understanding of other countries, cultures and societies;
- evaluative orientation: political education shall lead learners to reflection on social norms, including those of other societies than their own, in order to lead them to a capacity for political judgement; this

corresponds to the aims of FLT to lead learners to respect the norms of other societies and to evaluate them in an unprejudiced way;

- action orientation: both political education and FLT aim to instil in learners a disposition for engagement and interaction with others; in the case of FLT the 'others' are usually from another culture and society and the interaction is, psychologically if not sociologically, of a different kind, but is an extension of engagement with people in one's own society.

By establishing this link with political education, Doyé makes explicit the evaluative dimension which descriptions of knowledge, skills and attitudes frequently ignore. For, although attitudes are often included in statements of aims, they are defined in terms of readiness for engagement with otherness and the reduction of prejudice. The notion of an 'evaluative orientation' also includes appropriate 'unprejudiced' attitudes but goes further, by acknowledging the tendency to evaluate cultures, often through comparison with one's own, without imposing a particular perspective or set of values. On the other hand it does not encompass the reflexive dimension of ICC, i.e. the acquisition of a perspective on and analysis of the beliefs, meanings and behaviours of one's own society and the different groups within it. Yet this latter aspect of foreign language education is crucial not only to successful intercultural communication but also to the contribution of FLT to political education. FLT should lead to cognitive and evaluative orientation towards learners' own society, a relativisation of the taken-for-granted, and consequently to an action orientation.

Political education in this interpretation does not impose or recommend any particular set of values, any particular standpoint, but it is possible to argue that political education in FLT should do so. Starkey (1995) argues that an international standpoint is to be found in the concept of human rights and peace education, and Classen-Bauer (1989) has produced materials for classroom practice which make the link between FLT and peace studies real. Moreover, since peace education can also be pursued in other subjects taught in general education, there is potential for cross-curricular co-operation. Taking international standards of human rights as the base-line for evaluation is not of course a ready-made solution to the question of what standpoint should or could be recommended, since interpretations of human rights differ, but it provides a starting point for those teachers who feel that they need to offer their learners a rational approach to evaluations of the value systems of other cultures. This is particularly important for those who teach languages from societies with very different moral and ethical traditions, with respect to the treatment of women or children, for example. On the one hand teachers wish to reduce prejudiced and emotional evaluations; on the other hand their learners react strongly to the marked differences. A human rights standpoint offers a rationale for handling strong emotional responses.

However, not all language teachers feel comfortable with such an explicit political dimension of language and culture teaching. They may also see it as irrelevant to language teaching for children or even for other beginners, whatever their age, arguing that the subject matter introduced in the early stages of language teaching does not require an evaluative attitude. This view is more easily defended when teaching languages spoken in areas with similar moral, ethical and political traditions, as is the case of much foreign language teaching within Western Europe. The teaching of Spanish in France or German in Britain or English in the Netherlands does not present learners with radically different societies, whereas the teaching of Arabic or Chinese does. Even so, a realistic representation in teaching materials of the country in question can and should soon introduce learners to different social groups, including those of low status and disadvantage. This can problematise a society's treatment of all its social groups, and through a reflexive methodology, raise questions about each learner's own society and its attitude to disadvantaged groups. Such issues can be found implicitly in textbooks, and are sometimes made explicit. For example, in a textbook for teaching English as a foreign language in Germany, young learners are introduced to a fictional family of Pakistani origin living in the north of England. The story represents a well-known problem in such communities when the family moves to a predominantly white neighbourhood and experiences racial prejudice. The racial problems are made all the more explicit when the daughter of the family begins to date a white boy. Learners cannot read this story without becoming aware of racial tensions in Britain and, by comparison, in Germany (Doyé, 1991).

As well as illustrating the point about languages from the same tradition, this example is taken from a secondary school context where the learners are reaching a stage of development when moral issues can, and some would say must, be addressed, since this is a responsibility of institutions of general education. Outside the secondary school category, beginning language learners fall into two other broad categories: those in primary or even pre-primary education, and those in post-secondary and adult education, whose ages may range from 20 years to 70 years or beyond. The literature on teaching languages in the early years does not address culture teaching, still less the question of evaluative attitudes. Research in the teaching of geography suggests that young children's concepts of other countries, and therefore presumably of other cultures, do not develop as quickly as their ability to learn another linguistic code (cf. Byram, Morgan *et al.*, 1994). There is a need for research in the language classroom to confirm or otherwise the conclusions from geography and provide a more systematic base for formulating the cultural learning aims of language teaching in the early years.

The second group, adult learners, often have specific aims in their language learning, even at the beginning stage, which bring evaluative attitudes to the fore. Particularly where the languages involved are from very different traditions, the evaluative attitude is a major concern, whether it is addressed in the classroom and teaching materials or not. This being the case, language teachers need to be explicit and the reference point of international human rights is a useful one here too. It helps all language teachers and learners to avoid the trap of cultural relativism. It offers a possible basis, too, for the development of a concept of 'world citizenship' and 'global education' in the foreign language curriculum (Starkey, 1988).

Even where the issues are not political or moral, FL teaching within an institution of general education has a responsibility to develop a critical awareness of the values and significance of cultural practices in the other and one's own culture. In some educational traditions this may simply mean that FLT should amend its educational goals to correspond to those of other disciplines. In the Western European and North American tradition, FLT can gain important insights from Cultural Studies, where methods exist to ensure that analysis is critical and that the interpretation makes explicit its point of view (Byram, 1997a). In other traditions, the introduction of a critical analysis not only of the foreign language and culture but also of one's own, is a more difficult issue. The fear of Western values as embodied in English as a foreign language is evident, for example, in the educational goal of the Arab Gulf States discussed in Chapter 1, and in the debate about neo-colonialism in general. It is here that the definition of human rights might be felt to be too much in debt to western concepts, and a critical cultural awareness too alien to traditions of conformity and acceptance of authority, but Pennycook (1994) makes a strong argument for a critical pedagogy in the teaching of English as an international language.

I have argued in this section for a view of FLT which is more complex than a process of developing skills and knowledge. It is represented diagrammatically in the model proposed earlier in this chapter by placing 'Education' at the centre, and including political education and critical cultural awareness. I do not propose here to discuss the methodological implications, whether for example, there should be methods for treating the issues explicitly or by permeation. It is nonetheless clear that the focus will continue to be on teaching language and culture, out of which political and critical awareness should arise. Ideally, FLT will be conceived by both teachers and learners as, in the first instance, a means to attain competence in intercultural communication through learning a language and its relationship to the cultural practices and identities interlocutors bring to an interaction. It is for this reason too that it is necessary in the following section to examine the relationships of the knowledge, skills and attitudes discussed so far to the other aspects of intercultural communicative competence.

Relating Intercultural Competence to Communication

The model proposed earlier in this chapter already includes a communication dimension in the skill of 'interaction'. It does not specify however the modes involved. These could include interaction through an interpreter, for example, but the underlying assumption has been that the dominant mode will be through the individual's own use of a foreign language, mainly but not exclusively in the spoken mode.

I pointed out in Chapter 1 that there is a strong argument for the inclusion of non-verbal communication in a model of intercultural communication, and cited Poyatos's (1992) proposal that FLT should include training in non-verbal communication. This is clearly an element of interaction which is crucial, but the challenge to the dominance of the native speaker as model applies just as much here as it does to standards of verbal communication. It is, too, an area of cultural practices which should be the focus of the skills of discovery, interpretation and relating to otherness. For, as with other aspects of a culture, the provision of knowledge can be only introductory and focused on major aspects of non-verbal practices. It is more important that learners as intercultural speakers should acquire the skills which allow them to observe practices of non-verbal communication and to relate them to their own.

A second perspective introduced in Chapter 1, represented by Gudykunst (1994), emphasised especially the abilities to gather knowledge about another culture and the skills of empathy, management of anxiety and adaptability. In my model these characteristics are included in attitudes and skills of discovery, interpretation and relating. The criticism I made of Gudykunst's and similar models is that they pay little or no attention to linguistic competence. Neither does the sociological interactionist perspective also analysed in Chapter 1. The reason is essentially the same in both cases: the view that interaction within 'a culture' or a country is not different in principle from that involving another language. I argued that this view does not take into account social identities, ascripted by others and self-ascripted, nor the relationship of identities to language.

In addition to this, it is necessary to consider the relationship between the elements of my model and the partial competences identified in van Ek's language-based model also outlined in Chapter 1. His concepts of 'social competence', 'strategic' and 'socio-cultural competence' are included in my model and refined as a consequence of my replacing the native speaker by the concept of intercultural speaker. The three other dimensions, repeated here for ease of reference, need to be reappraised:

- *linguistic competence*: the ability to produce and interpret meaningful utterances which are formed in accordance with the rules of the language concerned and bear their conventional meaning ... that meaning which native speakers would normally attach to an utterance when used in isolation (p.39);
- *sociolinguistic competence*: the awareness of ways in which the choice of language forms ... is determined by such conditions as setting, relationship between communication partners, communicative intention, etc., etc. ... sociolinguistic competence covers the relation between linguistic signals and their contextual — or situational — meaning (p.41);
- *discourse competence*: the ability to use appropriate strategies in the construction and interpretation of texts (p.47).

Given the significance I have attached to 'discovery', 'interpretation' and 'establishing a relationship' between an intercultural speaker and the native speaker, who may have little intercultural competence, van Ek's definitions of linguistic, sociolinguistic and discourse competence need to be refined:

- *linguistic competence*: the ability to apply knowledge of the rules of a standard version of the language to produce and interpret spoken and written language;
- *sociolinguistic competence*: the ability to give to the language produced by an interlocutor — whether native speaker or not — meanings which are taken for granted by the interlocutor or which are negotiated and made explicit with the interlocutor;
- *discourse competence*: the ability to use, discover and negotiate strategies for the production and interpretation of monologue or dialogue texts which follow the conventions of the culture of an interlocutor or are negotiated as intercultural texts for particular purposes.

These formulations retain some of the insights of van Ek's model but imply links with the knowledge and skills of my model. The redefinition of linguistic competence to exclude reference to meaning involves a redefinition of sociolinguistic competence to include the taken for granted meanings learners might have acquired as knowledge of a foreign culture and the ability to discover and negotiate new and unfamiliar meanings, which may also diverge from those of the national culture at the focus of the learner's attention. Similarly the redefinition of discourse competence includes the notion of discovery and negotiation but also adds the possibility that intercultural and native speakers — or intercultural speakers of different language and culture origins — need to negotiate their own modes of interaction, their own kinds of text, to accommodate the specific nature of intercultural communication. This might involve, for example, negotiated agreements on meta-commentary, on when and how to ensure that each interlocutor is able to interrupt the normal flow of interaction to ask for explanation of differences and dysfunctions, or to give a richer account of the pre-suppositions of a statement than would usually be necessary.

The important point in all this is of course to note that there are significant connections between the partial competences which make up ICC. The definition of the intercultural speaker as distinct from the native speaker has consequences for all aspects of the competence involved. Nonetheless, I shall not discuss in further detail the linguistic, sociolinguistic and discourse dimensions but return to a more detailed specification of intercultural attitudes, skills and knowledge in a way which make them usable for teaching and assessment.

Intercultural Competence Defined in Terms of Objectives

By referring in this section to intercultural competence, omitting reference to communication, I want to indicate the emphasis on skills, knowledge and attitudes other than those which are primarily linguistic. It will be evident that the skill of 'interaction' is communicative in a broader sense, and that any comprehensive account of teaching and assessing ICC must include all the competences discussed in the previous section. Here I propose to return to the five factors in my model and extend the discussion of them in terms of how they might be formulated as 'objectives'.

The use of the term 'objectives' in discourse on education and learning is not consistent. The confusion is compounded if one includes discourse in languages other than English where the apparent translation is often understood in quite different ways. Here I shall use it to designate a range of skills, knowledge and attitudes which may not necessarily be the outcome of learning directly related to language learning, since they may include phenomena already present in the learner before language learning begins. Furthermore, the objectives need not necessarily be formulated as observable and measurable behaviours or changes in behaviour. To require this would be too restrictive in understanding language and culture learning, although it may be necessary later to reconsider this issue with respect to assessment. Finally, objectives are not limited to describing the intentions of the teacher or even of the learner in engaging in a process of language learning. 'Objectives' are thus a refinement of the definitions introduced earlier and a step towards describing teaching and assessment.[6]

Attitudes: *Curiosity and openness, readiness to suspend disbelief about other cultures and belief about one's own.*

Objectives:

- willingness to seek out or take up opportunities to engage with otherness in a relationship of equality; this should be distinguished from attitudes of seeking out the exotic or of seeking to profit from others;
- interest in discovering other perspectives on interpretation of familiar and unfamiliar phenomena both in one's own and in other cultures and cultural practices;
- willingness to question the values and presuppositions in cultural practices and products in one's own environment;
- readiness to experience the different stages of adaptation to and interaction with another culture during a period of residence;
- readiness to engage with the conventions and rites of verbal and non-verbal communication and interaction

What I have in mind here is the kind of learner many teachers will have noticed when they take a group to another country. It is the curiosity and wonder expressed in constant questions and wide-eyed observations, in the willingness to try anything new rather than cling to the familiar. In the classroom, these attitudes are sometimes evident in the willingness to improvise in using the language, or in the question at the end of a lesson about something noticed in a textbook, or in the learner who talks about what they have heard from relatives about another country. Among university students spending a period of residence in another country, there are those who become fully engaged with their environment rather then live almost encapsulated in the links with home. Often such learners are not the ones most successful in academic work, in the acquisition of linguistic accuracy in the classroom, for example.

I also want to distinguish this kind of engagement with otherness from the tourist approach where the interest is in collecting experiences of the exotic, and from the commercial approach where the interest is in a business arrangement and the making of a profit. Both of these have a rightful place in international relations, but they are not conducive to developing intercultural competence.

***Knowledge**: of social groups and their products and practices in one's own and in one's interlocutor's country, and of the general processes of societal and individual interaction.*

Objectives (knowledge about/of):

- historical and contemporary relationships between one's own and one's interlocutor's countries
- the means of achieving contact with interlocutors from another country (at a distance or in proximity), of travel to and from and the institutions which facilitate contact or help resolve problems
- the types of cause and process of misunderstanding between interlocutors of different cultural origins
- the national memory of one's own country and how its events are related to and seen from the perspective of one's interlocutor's country
- the national memory of one's interlocutor's country and the perspective on it from one's own
- the national definitions of geographical space in one's own country and how these are perceived from the perspective of other countries
- the national definitions of geographical space in one's interlocutor's country and the perspective on them from one's own
- the processes and institutions of socialisation in one's own and one's interlocutor's country
- social distinctions and their principal markers, in one's own country and one's interlocutor's
- institutions, and perceptions of them, which impinge on daily life within one's own and one's interlocutor's country and which conduct and influence relationships between them
- the processes of social interaction in one's interlocutor's country.

Much of the knowledge involved here is relational, e.g. how the inhabitants of one country perceive another country and what effect that has upon the interaction between individuals. It is also related to socialisation, since perceptions of others are acquired in socialisation. In learning the history of one's own country, for example, one is presented with images of another; in learning about the geography of one's own country, the boundaries with other countries are the defining characteristics. As an example, an English learner of French inevitably meets at some point the two versions of the story — rather than the history — of Joan of Arc. The French collective, national memory of this story is different from the English, and the historical relationships between the two countries encapsulated in the difference is the kind of knowledge envisaged here. There are doubtless similar examples in every country.

There is also a more theoretical kind of knowledge. Behind the example just mentioned, is the socialisation process itself, and an intercultural speaker needs to understand how this creates different perceptions, rather than having to acquire knowledge of all specific instances and examples. Awareness that one is a product of one's own socialisation is a pre-condition for understanding one's reactions to otherness. Similarly, awareness of how one's 'natural' ways of interacting with other people are the 'naturalised' product of socialisation, and how parallel but different modes of interaction can be expected in other cultures, is part of the knowledge an intercultural speaker needs.

Skills of interpreting and relating: *Ability to interpret a document or event from another culture, to explain it and relate it to documents from one's own.*

Objectives (ability to):

- identify ethnocentric perspectives in a document or event and explain their origins;
- identify areas of misunderstanding and dysfunction in an interaction and explain them in terms of each of the cultural systems present;
- mediate between conflicting interpretations of phenomena

Documents depicting another culture — television reports, tourist brochures, autobiographical travellers' tales, or even language learning textbooks — may honestly claim to give an 'impartial' or 'objective' account. Knowledge about the ways in which ethnocentric perspectives are acquired in socialisation is the basis for developing the skills of 'reading' such documents, and identifying the sometimes insidious and unconscious effects of ethnocentrism. Similarly, an intercultural speaker will notice how two people are misunderstanding each other because of their ethnocentrism, however linguistically competent they might be, and is able to identify and explain the pre-suppositions in a statement in order to reduce the dysfunction they cause.

Skills of discovery and interaction: *Ability to acquire new knowledge of a culture and cultural practices and the ability to operate knowledge, attitudes and skills under the constraints of real-time communication and interaction.*

Objectives (ability to):

- elicit from an interlocutor the concepts and values of documents or events and to develop an explanatory system susceptible of application to other phenomena;

- identify significant references within and across cultures and elicit their significance and connotations;
- identify similar and dissimilar processes of interaction, verbal and non-verbal, and negotiate an appropriate use of them in specific circumstances;
- use in real-time an appropriate combination of knowledge, skills and attitudes to interact with interlocutors from a different country and culture, taking into consideration the degree of one's existing familiarity with the country and culture and the extent of difference between one's own and the other;
- identify contemporary and past relationships between one's own and the other culture and country;
- identify and make use of public and private institutions which facilitate contact with other countries and cultures;
- use in real-time knowledge, skills and attitudes for mediation between interlocutors of one's own and a foreign culture.

These are the skills which enable some people quickly to establish an understanding of a new cultural environment and the ability to interact in increasingly rich and complex ways with people whose culture is unfamiliar to them. They are able to draw upon whatever knowledge they have but above all have the skills of the ethnographer entering into a new 'field' of study, whether in a remote community, a street-corner gang or the staffroom of a school. The foreign correspondent of newspaper or television is another example of someone who develops such skills, quickly discovering the streams of thought, power, influence underlying the events which they are to report. The intercultural speaker has different purposes from the ethnographer and the correspondent, but operates similar skills under similar constraints of time and place.

Critical cultural awareness/political education*: An ability to evaluate critically and on the basis of explicit criteria perspectives, practices and products in one's own and other cultures and countries.*

Objectives (ability to):

- identify and interpret explicit or implicit values in documents and events in one's own and other cultures;
- make an evaluative analysis of the documents and events which refers to an explicit perspective and criteria;
- interact and mediate in intercultural exchanges in accordance with explicit criteria, negotiating where necessary a degree of acceptance of them by drawing upon one's knowledge, skills and attitudes.

The important point here is that the intercultural speaker brings to the experiences of their own and other cultures a rational and explicit standpoint from which to evaluate. Teachers are familiar with learners of all ages who condemn some particular custom in another country as 'barbaric'. They have no rationale other than that of the original meaning of 'barbaric', i.e. that it is different and from beyond the limits of our 'civilised' society. Although the teacher may not wish to interfere in the views of their learners, for ethical reasons, they can encourage them to make the basis for their judgements explicit, and expect them to be consistent in their judgements of their own society as well as others.

The Developmental Factor

We saw earlier in this chapter that work on identifying degrees of intercultural communicative competence tends to focus in fact on degrees of incompetence, stages on the way to a threshold of competence. There is no work on defining further stages beyond a notional threshold.[7] We also saw that Melde and others have argued that the acquisition of attitudes and perspectives on otherness presupposes attainment of specific stages of psychological development, particularly in the domain of moral development. My definitions of skills and knowledge presuppose in some cases considerable capacity for the abstraction usually associated with attainment of a specific stage of cognitive development.

There is then an implicit judgement in this approach that individuals who do not, or have not yet attained particular stages of development are not able to become fully competent as defined. In the case of young people and adults it can be argued that appropriately structured experience of and reflection on otherness can help to develop levels of understanding and moral judgement not yet developed to their full potential. In the case of young children of primary school age whose development cannot yet be expected to support the knowledge, skills and attitudes defined here, it would be inappropriate to judge them to be incompetent. It is necessary, rather, to examine the nature of the contact they might have with others, of their own age and older, from a different culture, and define the nature of intercultural communicative competence in those terms. This an issue to which I shall return in a later chapter.

Notes

1. For the sake of clarity, I shall refer throughout to 'countries' when discussing inter-lingual and inter-cultural communication, although it is evident that other geo-political entities may be more relevant in some situations. I do not wish to imply by this that countries and nation-states are the inevitable entities of

linguistic and cultural allegiance, but they are currently dominant and are the basis on which education systems are usually organised. I would argue that *mutatis mutandis,* my discussion of intercultural communication can also apply to other geo-political entities, such as ethnic minorities with their own education systems.

2. I have used the literal translation of '*politische Bildung*', discussed later in this chapter, despite the difficulties this raises in the anglophone world with its fear of 'indoctrination'; other phrases are current, such as 'education for citizenship' in the UK or 'education for democracy' in the USA.
3. This is a development from earlier work (see below, note 6) and conserves the elegance of French terminology in which knowledge, skills and attitudes can be described as different *savoirs.*
4. It is likely that 'extrovert' personalities will cope with the demands of such situations more easily than 'introverts', but at this stage I am concerned with the competences involved rather than the question of aptitude.
5. This is not to deny that issues of power also exist within a country and culture, as has been shown by Fairclough (1989) for example, but the person who is struggling with a foreign language is more aware of the source of their difficulties than someone speaking their first language. It is precisely the value of Fairclough's and others' work that they uncover the power relationships of which speakers in their own culture and country are not aware.
6. This section draws heavily on Byram & Zarate (1994) and Byram (1993). See also Byram & Zarate (1996).
7. There is however unpublished work by Trim and van Ek for the Council of Europe which proposes a definition of a 'Vantage Level'.

Chapter 3
Objectives for Teaching, Learning and Assessment

Introduction

By the end of Chapter 2, I had proposed a model of ICC (comprising linguistic, sociolinguistic, discourse and intercultural components), discussed the factors involved in intercultural competence (skills, knowledge, attitudes and critical cultural awareness) and suggested how intercultural competence components can be formulated as 'objectives'.[1] I deliberately used this term in an open-ended way so as not to exclude factors simply because they might not correspond to existing notions of language learning. In this chapter, I shall attempt to refine the formulations in ways which bring them closer to activities undertaken by learners, teachers and assessors. I shall argue that objectives formulated in this way oblige us to envisage various modes and locations for learning and a variety of relationships between the three groups involved. A diagrammatic representation of all these different dimensions is provided and explained in the final section of this chapter, and readers may find it helpful to consult that section during the discussions of detail which are the main body of this chapter.

The purpose of this chapter is then to attempt to answer questions of principle which will provide the link between the definition of ICC, and in particular intercultural competence, and the planning of curricula and assessment. I do not propose in this book to make suggestions or give examples of teaching processes since, as argued in Chapter 1, these will be dependent on context. With respect to assessment, too, I propose in this chapter and later to discuss principles rather than case-studies of practice, whether in classrooms or other locations.[2]

Formulating Teaching, Learning and Assessment Objectives

The advantages to be gained from the formulation of objectives are those of comprehensiveness, coherence and transparency (cf. Council of Europe, 1993) as well as precision. The formulation should ensure that all aspects of ICC are included (comprehensiveness), that their relationship to each other is made evident (coherence) and that they can be understood and agreed by all involved — the three groups mentioned earlier and also educational planners and policy makers. The search for precision is of particular value in the detailed planning of curricula and the realisation of curricula in teaching, learning and assessment processes. Precision is often sought by defining objectives in terms of observable behaviours on the part of learners, behaviours which can also be measured. It is assumed that the observation and measurement should be by someone other than the learner and might even exclude the teacher. Furthermore the measurement should be in terms of objective quantification. An alternative approach is to replace quantification of observations with qualitative characterisations of behaviour related to agreed criteria (criterion-referenced assessment). This retains the role of the external observer, who might for example be the teacher attempting to verify the efficacy of their teaching by looking for changes in behaviour. A further refinement is to allow the learner to check their own behaviour against agreed criteria, perhaps with the help of another learner, but nonetheless retaining some external qualitative measure and encouraging the learner to reflect as an outsider on their own performance.

I propose, at least initially, to ignore the constraints of defining objectives always in behavioural terms externally observable and always measurable. In order to make the definitions of objectives proposed in Chapter 2 more precise, I shall ask the question: 'What might count as ...' about those objectives, irrespective of whether the answer is in terms of observable behaviours. In doing so it becomes clear that the relationship between skills, attitudes and knowledge discussed in Chapter 2 leads to overlap and repetition among objectives' descriptions. This would clearly also be the case with more precise descriptions of linguistic, sociolinguistic and discourse competences. Actual performances would make this even more evident, as the various competences are integrated in real-time interaction (*savoir apprendre/faire*).

Attitudes: *curiosity and openness, readiness to suspend disbelief about other cultures and belief about one's own.*

Objectives:

(a) willingness to seek out or take up opportunities to engage with otherness in a relationship of equality, distinct from seeking out the exotic or the profitable.

The intercultural speaker is interested in the other's experience of daily life in contexts not usually presented to outsiders through the media nor used to develop a commercial relationship with outsiders;

is interested in the daily experience of a range of social groups within a society and not only that represented in the dominant culture.

(b) interest in discovering other perspectives on interpretation of familiar and unfamiliar phenomena both in one's own and in other cultures and cultural practices

The intercultural speaker does not assume that familiar phenomena —cultural practices or products common to themselves and the other —are understood in the same way, or that unfamiliar phenomena can only be understood by assimilating them to their own cultural phenomena; and is aware that they need to discover the other person's understanding of these, and of phenomena in their own culture which are not familiar to the other person.

(c) willingness to question the values and presuppositions in cultural practices and products in one's own environment

The intercultural speaker actively seeks the other's perspectives and evaluations of phenomena in the intercultural speaker's environment which are taken for granted, and takes up the other's perspectives in order to contrast and compare with the dominant evaluations in their own society.

(d) readiness to experience the different stages of adaptation to and interaction with another culture during a period of residence

The intercultural speaker is able to cope with their own different kinds of experience of otherness (e.g. enthusiasm, withdrawal) during residence and place them in a longer term context of phases of acceptance and rejection.

(e) readiness to engage with the conventions and rites of verbal and non-verbal communication and interaction

The intercultural speaker notes and adopts the behaviours specific to a social group in a way which they and the members of that group consider to be appropriate for an outsider; the intercultural speaker takes into consideration the expectations the others may have about appropriate behaviour from foreigners.

Knowledge: *of social groups and their products and practices in one's own and in one's interlocutor's country, and of the general processes of societal and individual interaction.*

Objectives (knowledge of/about):

(a) historical and contemporary relationships between one's own and one's interlocutor's countries

The intercultural speaker knows about events, significant individuals and diverse interpretations of events which have involved both countries and the traces left in the national memory; and about political and economic factors in the contemporary alliances of each country.

(b) the means of achieving contact with interlocutors from another country (at a distance or in proximity), of travel to and from, and the institutions which facilitate contact or help resolve problems

The intercultural speaker knows about (and how to use) telecommunications, consular and similar services, modes and means of travel, and public and private organisations which facilitate commercial, cultural/leisure and individual partnerships across frontiers.

(c) the types of cause and process of misunderstanding between interlocutors of different cultural origins

The intercultural speaker knows about conventions of communication and interaction in their own and the foreign cultures, about the unconscious effects of paralinguistic and non-verbal phenomena, about alternative interpretations of shared concepts, gestures, customs and rituals.

(d) the national memory of one's own country and how its events are related to and seen from the perspective of other countries

The intercultural speaker knows the events and their emblems (myths, cultural products, sites of significance to the collective memory) which are markers of national identity in one's own country as they are portrayed in public institutions and transmitted through processes of socialisation, particularly those experienced in schools; and is aware of other perspectives on those events.

(e) the national memory of one's interlocutor's country and the perspective on them from one's own country

The intercultural speaker knows about the national memory of the other in the same way as their own (see above).

(f) the national definitions of geographical space in one's own country, and how these are perceived from the perspective of other countries

The intercultural speaker knows about perceptions of regions and regional identities, of language varieties (particularly regional dialects and languages), of landmarks of significance, of markers of internal and external borders and frontiers, and how these are perceived by others.

(g) the national definitions of geographical space in one's interlocutor's country and the perspective on them from one's own

The intercultural speaker knows about perceptions of space in the other country as they do about their own (see above).

(h) the processes and institutions of socialisation in one's own and one's interlocutor's country

The intercultural speaker knows about education systems, religious institutions, and similar locations where individuals acquire a national identity, are introduced to the dominant culture in their society, pass through specific rites marking stages in the life-cycle, in both their own and the other country.

(i) social distinctions and their principal markers, in one's own country and one's interlocutor's

The intercultural speaker knows about the social distinctions dominant in the two countries — e.g. those of social class, ethnicity, gender, profession, religion — and how these are marked by visible phenomena such as clothing or food, and invisible phenomena such as language variety — e.g. minority languages, and socially determined accent — or non-verbal behaviour, or modes of socialisation and rites of passage.

(j) institutions, and perceptions of them, which impinge on daily life within one's own and one's interlocutor's country and which conduct and influence relationships between them

The intercultural speaker knows about public or private institutions which affect the living conditions of the individual in the two countries — e.g. with respect to health, recreation, financial situation, access to information in the media, access to education.

(k) the processes of social interaction in one's interlocutor's country

The intercultural speaker knows about levels of formality in the language and non-verbal behaviour of interaction, about conventions of behaviour and beliefs and taboos in routine situations such as meals, different forms of public and private meeting, public behaviour such as use of transport etc.

***Skills of interpreting and relating**: ability to interpret a document or event from another culture, to explain it and relate it to documents or events from one's own.*

Objectives (ability to):

(a) identify ethnocentric perspectives in a document or event and explain their origins

The intercultural speaker: can 'read' a document or event, analysing its origins/sources — e.g. in the media, in political speech or historical writing — and the meanings and values which arise from a national or other ethnocentric perspective (stereotypes, historical connotations in texts) and which are presupposed and implicit, leading to conclusions which can be challenged from a different perspective.

(b) identify areas of misunderstanding and dysfunction in an interaction and explain them in terms of each of the cultural systems present

The intercultural speaker can identify causes of misunderstanding (e.g. use of concepts apparently similar but with different meanings or connotations; use of genres in inappropriate situations; introduction of topics inappropriate to a context, etc.) and dysfunctions (e.g. unconscious response to unfamiliar non-verbal behaviour, proxemic and paralanguage phenomena; over-generalisation from examples; mistaken assumptions about representativeness of views expressed); and can explain the errors and their causes by reference to knowledge of each culture involved.

(c) mediate between conflicting interpretations of phenomena

The intercultural speaker can use their explanations of sources of misunderstanding and dysfunction to help interlocutors overcome conflicting perspectives; can explain the perspective of each and the origins of those perspectives in terms accessible to the other; can help interlocutors to identify common ground and unresolvable difference.

***Skills of discovery and interaction**: ability to acquire new knowledge of a culture and cultural practices and the ability to operate knowledge, attitudes and skills under the constraints of real-time communication and interaction.*

Objectives (ability to):

(a) elicit from an interlocutor the concepts and values of documents or events and develop an explanatory system susceptible of application to other phenomena

The intercultural speaker can use a range of questioning techniques to elicit from informants the allusions, connotations and presuppositions of a document or event and their origins/sources, and can develop and test generalisations about shared meanings and values (by using them to interpret another document; by questioning another informant; by consulting appropriate literature) and establish links and relationships among them (logical relationships of hierarchy, of cause and effect, of conditions and consequence, etc.).

(b) identify significant references within and across cultures and elicit their significance and connotations

The intercultural speaker can 'read' a document or event for the implicit references to shared meanings and values (of national memory, of concepts of space, of social distinction, etc.) particular to the culture of their interlocutor, or of international currency (arising for example from the dominance of western satellite television); in the latter case, the intercultural speaker can identify or elicit different interpretations and connotations and establish relationships of similarity and difference between them.

(c) identify similar and dissimilar processes of interaction, verbal and non-verbal, and negotiate an appropriate use of them in specific circumstances

The intercultural speaker can use their knowledge of conventions of verbal and non-verbal interaction (of conversational structures; of formal communication such as presentations; of written correspondence; of business meetings; of informal gatherings, etc.) to establish agreed procedures on specific occasions, which may be a combination of conventions from the different cultural systems present in the interaction.

(d) use in real-time an appropriate combination of knowledge, skills and attitudes to interact with interlocutors form a different country and culture taking into consideration the degree of one's existing familiarity with the country, culture and language and the extent of difference between one's own and the other

The intercultural speaker is able to estimate their degree of proximity to the language and culture of their interlocutor (closely related cultures; cultures with little or no contact or little or no shared experience of international phenomena; cultures sharing the 'same' language; cultures with unrelated languages) and to draw accordingly on skills of interpreting, discovering, relating different assumptions and presuppositions or connotations in order to ensure understanding and avoid dysfunction.

(e) identify contemporary and past relationships between one's own and the other culture and society

The intercultural speaker can use sources (e.g. reference books, newspapers, histories, experts, lay informants) to understand both contemporary and historical political, economic and social relationships between cultures and societies and analyse the differing interpretations involved.

(f) identify and make use of public and private institutions which facilitate contact with other countries and cultures

The intercultural speaker can use their general knowledge of institutions facilitating contacts to identify specific institutions (consulates, cultural institutes, etc.) to establish and maintain contacts over a period of time.

(g) use in real-time knowledge, skills and attitudes for mediation between interlocutors of one's own and a foreign culture

The intercultural speaker can identify and estimate the significance of misunderstandings and dysfunctions in a particular situation and is able to decide on and carry out appropriate intervention, without disrupting interaction and to the mutual satisfaction of the interlocutors.

Critical cultural awareness/political education*: an ability to evaluate, critically and on the basis of explicit criteria, perspectives, practices and products in one's own and other cultures and countries.*

Objectives (ability to):

(a) identify and interpret explicit or implicit values in documents and events in one's own and other cultures

The intercultural speaker: can use a range of analytical approaches to place a document or event in context (of origins/sources, time, place, other documents or events) and to demonstrate the ideology involved.

(b) make an evaluative analysis of the documents and events which refers to an explicit perspective and criteria

The intercultural speaker is aware of their own ideological perspectives and values ('human rights'; socialist; liberal; Moslem; Christian etc.) and evaluates documents or events with explicit reference to them.

(c) interact and mediate in intercultural exchanges in accordance with explicit criteria, negotiating where necessary a degree of acceptance of those exchanges by drawing upon one's knowledge, skills and attitudes

The intercultural speaker is aware of potential conflict between their own and other ideologies and is able to establish common criteria of evaluation of documents or events, and where this is not possible because of incompatibilities in belief and value systems, is able to negotiate agreement on places of conflict and acceptance of difference.

Acquiring Intercultural Competence

Describing the objectives of intercultural competence more precisely makes it evident that they are very demanding and more complex than those which usually guide the work done in classrooms. It is clear that some objectives can be introduced as curriculum development, for example, those of discovery skills, but others may not be compatible with classroom work as usually conceived. Furthermore, it should be noted that teachers whose professional identity is that of the linguist, educated in a tradition of philology or linguistics, may find the range of objectives introduced here difficult to accept. On the other hand, teachers whose professional identity includes an education in literary criticism, will probably find analogies in the skills of interpreting and discovering with the traditions of some approaches to literature. These are important issues of teacher training and education which are being addressed elsewhere (Byram, 1994; Sercu, 1995; Kramsch, 1993; Zarate *et al.*, 1996; Byram, in press b).

The limitations of the classroom can be overcome to some degree by learning beyond the classroom walls, where the teacher still has a role. As FLT is increasingly seen as linked with education for mobility, there is a corresponding interest in visits, exchanges and other forms of contact, both real and virtual, using contemporary and projected technology. The teacher can structure and influence the learning opportunities involved, even when not physically present. The aim may be, for example, to develop learner autonomy within a structured and framed experience of otherness outside the classroom. It is then a short step to experiences of otherness without the involvement of the teacher, through independent vacations or periods of residence, through exchanges whose main purpose is not pedagogical, for example in town-twinning. The learner who has acquired autonomy in learning can use and improve their intercultural competence through performance. Furthermore, as we take more seriously the concept of life-long learning and the notion of 'the Learning Society' (European Commission, 1996), the significance of self-directed learning in engagement with otherness becomes all the more evident.[3]

There are thus three broad and overlapping categories of location for acquiring intercultural competence: the classroom, the pedagogically structured experience outside the classroom, the independent experience. In order to pursue the purpose of this chapter, i.e. to clarify the roles of learners, teachers and assessors and to provide principles for planning curriculum and assessment, I shall relate the different categories of location to the objectives described above.

The classroom

The traditional emphasis in cultural learning in the classroom has been on the acquisition of knowledge about another country and culture. In the worst case, this involves decontextualised factual information with minimal relationship to the language learning focus at a given moment. In better scenarios, information is structured according to principles developed from sociological or cultural anthropological analysis and linked to the acquisition of language. Clearly the classroom has advantages. It provides the space for systematic and structured presentation of knowledge in prolongation of the better traditions of language teaching. In addition it can offer the opportunity for acquisition of skills under the guidance of a teacher. Thirdly, the classroom can be the location for reflection on skills and knowledge acquisition beyond the classroom walls, and therefore for the acquisition of attitudes towards that which has been experienced.

Of course there is usually an assumption that classroom learning is in preparation for experience 'in the real world' and 'later', but in contrast to that view I want to suggest that engagement with otherness in the contemporary world is simultaneous — through the media on a daily basis, through occasional visiting and receiving visitors, or working and learning together with people of another culture. This means that the dichotomy of 'classroom' and 'real world' is a false one; the learning process is integrated and can be structured; learners do not metamorphose on the threshold of the classroom. Thus one of the crucial issues is deciding what the nature of the relationship should be between learning inside and outside the classroom, for it is not simply a question of classroom theory and real world practice, or 'pure' and 'applied' knowledge.

Let us consider the knowledge dimension first. One significant feature in the definition of objectives is knowledge of relationships: relationships among different perceptions of one's own and another culture, and secondly, relationships in the processes of individual and societal interaction. This should be the focus of classroom teaching. With reference to objectives involving knowledge of one's own and other cultures, for example knowledge of 'national memory', learners need to know not only about the emblems, myths and other features of national memory in both countries but also about mutual perspectives on them (*'le regard croisé'*). Some learners will be already familiar with their own country's national memory and others will be in the process of acquiring it. Some will have knowledge already of features of another country's national memory and others will have none. The precise nature of the curriculum therefore depends on learners' needs. In the case of children, the FL teacher may need to co-operate with other teachers to develop learners' knowledge of the national memory of their own country. Teachers of adult learners can usually assume greater familiarity of learners' own and the other culture. In both cases however the focus should be on the relationships between cultures, which implies a comparative method (cf. Byram, Morgan *et al.*, 1994; Byram & Zarate, 1995).

The classroom is also the place where learners can gain knowledge of the processes of intercultural communication. There is a link with knowledge about mutual perceptions between countries and cultures since these are the bases of international relationships. For example, as learners are introduced to features of the national memory of another country, how they are perceived in its dominant culture and how they are perceived by other societies including their own, they acquire knowledge of presuppositions which influence communication. The development of this involves knowledge about other dimensions of communication which may produce dysfunctions. These include non-verbal processes, knowledge of which can be acquired through analysis of examples of communication breakdown. They also include taboos, on topics of communication or on proxemic behaviour for example.

The advantage of placing relationships at the focus of knowledge teaching is that they are more easily linked to communication and the acquisition of language. On the other hand, the enumeration of areas of significance in the definition of objectives ensures that the learner acquires a systematic knowledge and not one which is simply the outcome of other factors such as the choice of teaching materials dominated by a linguistic syllabus.

The classroom also provides opportunities for teaching the skills of interpreting and relating documents or events. Knowledge and skill are inter-related ('know that' and 'know how') and the classroom allows teachers and learners to practise and reflect upon the skills of 'reading' a document — or an event in a document such as a video-recording — in a time dimension where the pressures of interaction can be neutralised. Skills of interpreting and relating draw upon knowledge, and methods need to be devised which combine the two in pedagogically appropriate ways, as illustrated in some textbooks (e.g. *'Typisch Deutsch?'*; *'Sprachbrücke'*; *'Sichtwechsel'*).[4] These skills can also be linked with the skill of discovery. Although the latter includes objectives of 'eliciting from an interlocutor the concepts and values of documents and events' which presupposes personal contact, that contact need not be outside the classroom. The techniques of telecommunications can bring immediate communication into the classroom, through electronic mail, fax, or video-conferencing, and the less immediate exchange of information through international mail can bring both textual data and other artefacts into the classroom (Jones, 1995). In all cases, the advantage of the classroom is that learners can acquire under the guidance of the teacher the skills of eliciting meanings, and can reflect on the efficacy of their attempts to do so. It is also possible for the teacher to provide data collected from sources 'in the field' as many teachers already do, but with a focus on finding data which is useful for exercising these skills rather than giving information. Telecommunications are not yet available to everyone but are not essential either.

A common factor in the teaching of skills and knowledge is the potential for reflection which the classroom offers by virtue of the teacher's control over the factor of time. Even the interaction by telecommunication can be slowed down to the timescale of the classroom if necessary. So the classroom has a potential for two kinds of relationship with learning outside: a prospective relationship of developing skills in anticipation of learning through fieldwork, and a retrospective relationship in which learners can reflect on learning in the field. This critical reflection is particularly important and can focus on the efficacy of the skills learned in the classroom, and the need for further development. It can also focus on learners' affective responses to learning outside the classroom, for example, in response to media representations of otherness or in response to the complex experience of visiting or residing in another country and culture. This suggests that the teacher has a role to play in realising the attitude objectives discussed earlier. Although this role is unlikely to be one of systematising and structuring learning in a way similar to the teaching of cultural knowledge or skills of discovery and interpretation, teachers and learners together can again take advantage of the time-frame of the classroom to reflect upon the experiences they have had in real-time interaction. This differs from learners simply discussing or giving expression to emotions outside the classroom in discussion with friends and family, because it is the teacher's responsibility to bear in mind the attitude and educational objectives of ICC and develop methods which help to realise them.

What the classroom cannot usually offer is the opportunity to develop the skills of interaction in real time. There are opportunities for rehearsal and, with respect to linguistic competence, it is possible to simulate real communication and performance (Hawkins, 1987). In some learning situations, such as some immersion or bilingual programmes, learners may also find themselves interacting with someone from another country and culture. In these cases, there can be real time intercultural communication, combined with reflection, analysis and skills development in the 'suspended' time of the classroom. In many foreign language as opposed to second language classrooms, however, this would be an exceptional experience, where there are interlocutors from another culture living in the same area. The teacher needs the opportunities offered by a visit to another country.

Fieldwork

I want to distinguish 'fieldwork' from 'independent' experience of otherness outside the classroom. In fieldwork, there is a pedagogical structure and educational objectives determined by the teacher often in consultation with learners. Fieldwork may be a short visit organised by a teacher for a group of learners, who continue to work as a class with their teacher. It can also be long-term period of residence organised for and by an individual learner who has limited or no contact with the teacher or other learners during the stay, but the fieldwork has nonetheless a prospective and retrospective relationship with the classroom. In this second example classroom learning is likely to be separated in time and space from fieldwork, but in cases where teacher and learners are together in the field they can also work simultaneously in the classroom, and the relationship between classroom and field is all the more close (cf. Dark *et al.*, 1997; Snow & Byram, 1997).

Fieldwork clearly allows the development of all the skills in real time, particularly the skill of interaction. It allows learners to bring their knowledge of relationships to bear on specific situations, and to discover and interpret new data. When those new data also lead to a generalisable system of explanation, learners continually add to the knowledge base provided in classroom learning. In interaction, learners have the opportunity to experience communication under time pressures, and in particular the significance of non-verbal behaviour. None of these need be left to chance, however, and the responsibility of the teacher to provide a pedagogical structure and systematic experience is what differentiates fieldwork from independent experience. The methodology involved and the evident need for teacher training and education for fieldwork are not the focus here but have been treated elsewhere (Alix & Bertrand, 1994; Byram & Zarate, 1995; Byram 1997b).

Perhaps the most significant advantage of fieldwork is in the context of attitude objectives. The experience of a total environment affecting all five senses challenges learners in ways which the classroom can seldom imitate. Experience of fieldwork, particularly over a longer term where learners are separated from other learners and teachers, and from their family and friends, provides them with the opportunity to develop attitudes which include ability to cope with different stages of adaptation, engagement with unfamiliar conventions of behaviour and interaction, and an interest in other cultures which is not that of the tourist or business person. This experience does not necessarily lead to learning, however, unless it is related to the reflection and analysis of the classroom (Kolb, 1984). It is here that the teacher's role in attitude objectives is important. In the classroom, the unconscious responses to otherness which are important in attitude development, can be made evident and isolated for reflection. Here again there are implications for teacher training (Francesconi & di Fasano, 1994; Poulain, 1997; Salvadori, 1997).

Independent learning

Independent learning is a factor in life-long learning and can be both subsequent to and simultaneous with classroom and fieldwork. It will be effective only if learners are able to continue to reflect upon as well as develop their knowledge, skills and attitudes, as a consequence of previous training. Otherwise, experience of otherness in one's own environment or in another country remains mere experience. For experience to become learning, learners must become autonomous in their capacity for refining and increasing their knowledge, skills and attitudes. This in turn suggests a classroom methodology which allows learners to acquire explicitly the underlying principles of the skills and knowledge they are taught, and the means of generalising them to new experience. In that case one could properly speak of a learning biography and expect that far more cultural learning will take place outside the classroom than inside, whether consecutively or simultaneously. If this were the case, then issues of assessment change too. Assessment would have to include all learning, whether inside or beyond the classroom, and the basic question would be what learning has taken place, rather than whether what has been taught in the classroom or in fieldwork has been acquired.

A Comprehensive Model of Intercultural Communicative Competence

We have come to a point where the definition phase is almost complete, and where the model proposed at a general and abstract level raises questions about approaches to teaching and assessment. As suggested in the discussion of the locations for cultural learning, the implications are far-reaching and concern teaching methods, modes of learning, teacher training and education, curriculum design and assessment. The purpose of this monograph is to address the latter two but before turning to these issues in more detail, I shall summarise the model and its purposes.

There are three fundamental features of the model of ICC:

- it proposes an attainable ideal, the intercultural speaker, and rejects the notion of the native speaker as a model for foreign language learners;
- it is a model for the acquisition of ICC in an educational context, and includes educational objectives;
- because it has an educational dimension, it includes specifications of locations of learning and of the roles of the teacher and learner.

The model is intended to be comprehensive, i.e. a rich description of ICC and the intercultural speaker which corresponds to the needs and opportunities of a foreign language learner with personal experience of interaction with people of another culture involving the use of a foreign language. It is also inclusive of other kinds of interaction — receiving a foreigner in one's own environment whilst speaking one's own language, or interaction through telecommunications for example — where only some of the competences included in the model are required.

It is thus possible to distinguish Intercultural Competence from Intercultural Communicative Competence. In the first case, individuals have the ability to interact in their own language with people from another country and culture, drawing upon their knowledge about intercultural communication, their attitudes of interest in otherness and their skills in interpreting, relating and discovering, i.e. of overcoming cultural difference and enjoying intercultural contact. Their ability to do this will probably derive from their experience of language learning, even though they do not use the specific language on a given occasion. A second example might be the individual's ability to interpret a translated document from another culture, which does not require knowledge of the language but does involve the skills of interpreting and relating, some knowledge about the other culture, and attitudes of interest and engagement. There is a link here with the teaching of foreign literature in translation, and other examples would be legal pronouncements, business agreements, dubbed television programmes or even kitchen recipes. It can be argued that language teaching should include these kinds of engagement with otherness as an aim and ensure an appropriate method which makes the value of intercultural competence apparent.

On the other hand, someone with Intercultural *Communicative* Competence is able to interact with people from another country and culture in a foreign language. They are able to negotiate a mode of communication and interaction which is satisfactory to themselves and the other and they are able to act as mediator between people of different cultural origins. Their knowledge of another culture is linked to their language competence through their ability to use language appropriately — sociolinguistic and discourse competence — and their awareness of the specific meanings, values and connotations of the language. They also have a basis for acquiring new languages and cultural understandings as a consequence of the skills they have acquired in the first.

The relationship between Intercultural Competence and Intercultural Communicative Competence is one of degrees of complexity and the ability to deal with a wider range of situations of contact in the latter than in the former. Decisions about which factors should be included in teaching aims cannot be made in the abstract but depend on circumstances and on the needs and opportunities of the learners involved. In both kinds of competence, however, educational objectives are included and this reflects the fact that most language learning takes place, or at least begins, in educational contexts. The model does not therefore depend on a concept of neutral communication of information across cultural barriers, but rather on a rich definition of communication as interaction, and on a philosophy of critical engagement with otherness and critical reflection on self.

There are corollaries of this educational dimension. The first is the need to include consideration of the locations where ICC is acquired and I have argued that there are three categories: classroom, fieldwork and independent learning, each of which is differently linked to the objectives of the model. The teacher and learner have differing roles and relationships in each of these. The second issue is related to the argument that the aim should be the intercultural and not the native speaker, which includes the view that this aim can be and often is attained. Two questions have been raised in the earlier discussion: whether it is appropriate and feasible to identify levels of proficiency beyond a 'threshold' of ICC; and second whether a particular level of cognitive development is a precondition for attainment of ICC. The second is significant in educational contexts where young children are acquiring ICC and suggests that a different kind of ICC has to be expected from young children who have not yet reached an age where the required level of cognitive development can be expected. The first question, about levels of proficiency, becomes particularly significant in educational contexts where institutions are expected to assess and certificate learners. Neither of these points can be introduced to a general and abstract model, for they are examples of issues which arise in specific circumstances. They are nonetheless indicative of questions to be treated in following chapters.

Figure 3.1 which provides a summary of the model remains biased towards the explication of the details of the cultural competence factors. It does not attempt to provide the same detail for the factors involved in language competence, although they are represented. Nor does it attempt to represent in two dimensions the complexity of the relationships among all the factors. On the other hand it includes a summary of the locations where ICC can be acquired in order to reflect my emphasis on the educational dimension.

Notes

1. The terms 'competence' and 'objectives' are notorious in the literature on education and curriculum analysis. It will have been evident in earlier chapters that I have used the term 'competence' in a sense derived from Chomsky and Hymes and my definition of intercultural competence includes knowledge, attitudes and skills. However, it is important as we approach questions of curriculum design and assessment to make explicit that I am not using them in the sense developed by the literature on performance objectives and competence-based curricula. I criticised the narrowness of this work, which can be traced to the behaviourism that Chomsky refuted, in an analysis of performance objectives in language teaching in the 1970s (Byram, 1978, 1979), and I fully accept the critique of more recent manifestations in the British education system by Hyland (1993).
2. In Byram, Morgan *et al.* 1994 we provided case-studies, including lesson descriptions and experiments in assessment techniques, from a number of different contexts.
3. The learning biographies of significant numbers of people in contemporary Western societies routinely include exchanges during formal education, tourism in other countries, visits in the framework of town-twinning and youth exchanges, and the reverse of these: receiving visitors, meeting tourists, working

with immigrants. The potential for improving the quality of learning in such experiences has yet to be properly explored.

4. *Typisch Deutsch?* (Behal-Thomsen *et al.*, 1993) is a workbook and excellent example of a comparative method of teaching German language and culture to Americans. For example, it includes techniques for comparison of culturally specific concepts of space and time, or 'private' and 'public'. *Sichtwechsel* (Bachman *et al.*, 1995) is a similar workbook containing techniques for developing learners' ability to decentre and to take a different perspective on the familiar through the new, 'making the familiar strange'. *Sprachbrücke* (Mebus *et al.*, 1987) is a textbook which includes methods of encouraging learners to think about how different cultures are experienced and how individuals can learn to cope with them.

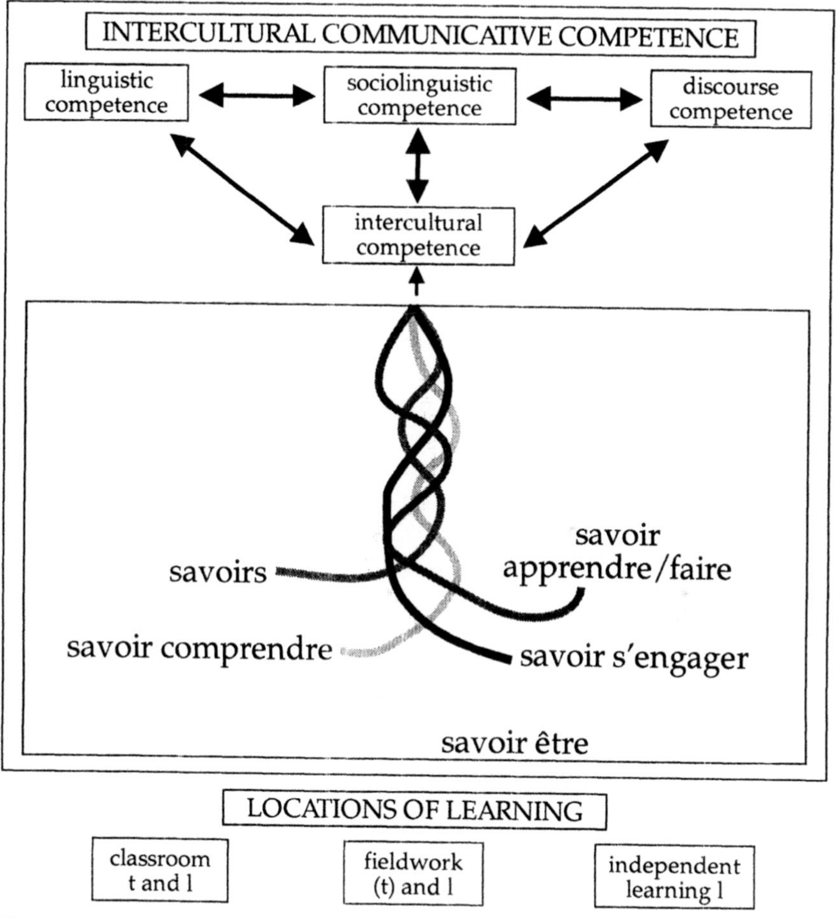

Figure 3.1

Chapter 4

Curriculum Issues

Introduction

In order to move from a model of ICC to the question of assessment, we need to consider the relationship between assessment and curriculum, and between curricular aims and the definition of ICC and its component parts. It is of course possible to argue that one can move directly from definitions of objectives to assessment, if one takes the view that the purpose of assessment is only to establish and possibly certificate proficiency. However, the view I have taken and the model proposed include educational objectives as an integral part of ICC, with a specific role for the FL teacher and this requires a curriculum in which the teacher's role can be realised. The teacher may then also have the role of assessor, either providing formative feedback to the learner, or determining the learner's level of attainment at the end of a course, or both.

The introduction of the concept of a curriculum puts a further responsibility on the teacher: to determine the order in which learners encounter and hopefully acquire different aspects of ICC. This responsibility is usually shared with others: with curriculum designers who provide a more or less detailed framework; with other teachers and with writers of teaching materials; with learners who specify their needs and interests. The curriculum is therefore more than a syllabus — both terms are frequently used in a variety of ways — in that a syllabus is a list of what is to be taught, sometimes including a list of appropriate materials, whereas a curriculum involves a proposal for ordering what is to be taught in order to arrive at specific objectives, which may themselves be ordered and integrated into the curriculum.[1]

Since I have argued that FLT is context-dependent, it is not possible to define either a curriculum for all situations, or a means of assessment. Therefore what I intend here is to identify the issues involved, examine some existing curricula, and distil some principles for curriculum design for ICC, always bearing in mind the goal of discussing the assessment of ICC which will be the subject of the following chapter.

Concepts of Progression

In FLT, progression in learning is usually thought of as linear and cumulative, with each stage depending on preceding ones, 'a journey or pilgrim's progress, a series of steps up a mountain, a straight and narrow path beset with difficulties and dangers, towards a distant goal which few but the truly devoted ever reach' (Trim, 1978: 5), the early steps being easier than later ones. The images arise from ways of ordering the grammar of a language in pedagogically appropriate ways, some of which are intuitive or claim to be logical, others related to anticipated use of the language by learners, others derived from the order of learning by native speakers, and others again appearing to arise from the structures of the language. Moreover, a pedagogical grammar may involve simplification of language structures in the early stages of learning, returning to present the full complexity at a later stage. In fact, it is only at the earlier stages of learning that the notion of each step depending on previous ones is evident. At later stages, the image of climbing a ladder can be replaced by the metaphor of completing a jigsaw puzzle, where the early stages have provided the edges and corners and at later stages learners, sometimes with the help of teachers, gradually complete elements of the whole picture without necessarily making connections among them until the picture is complete.

The concept of step-by-step progression is also evident in currently dominant modes of assessment where a quantified scale suggests progress upwards. Those higher up the scale know the same as those lower down, and more. For certification they are considered to be better qualified than those lower down; the metaphor of the ladder for the scaling of qualifications (in French the same word is used) is reinforced in some cases by the names of certificates (Scottish 'Highers'). This approach serves well the requirements of societies, namely that certificates should be used for allocating individuals to positions in the economy, and then in society as a whole — the gate-keeping function.

The objections to this view of progression include one from the learning perspective and one from the perspective on definitions of what is to be learnt. Briefly, the former suggests that learning is not necessarily linear and step-by-step (Gipps, 1994). Learners often need to revisit issues and encounter them in different contexts and perspectives. Furthermore their needs may suggest a different order from that usually taken, and their needs may change and require different priorities at different points in their learning process, particularly when that process is life-long. A particularly important aspect of this perspective is the question of the cognitive development of young learners, discussed in the preceding chapter. For both teaching and assessment purposes, it can be argued that some aspects of ICC, though in definitional terms fundamental, cannot be acquired by young learners and therefore should be omitted.

From the perspective afforded by definitions, I have argued that each component of intercultural competence is inter-related with others, and with language competences in ICC. This excludes the possibility of presenting one before others, knowledge before skills for example. I have also argued that, according to circumstances, some components may be given less emphasis or ignored because they are and will not be required, and this view excludes the notion of requiring equal competence in all components to qualify for a certificate at a given level in one education system or across education systems. With respect to assessment for certification, the alternative solution of giving equal status to different combinations of competences within ICC, and perhaps to different levels within the combinations, is an issue to which I shall return in the next chapter.

Another issue raised in the earlier discussion of definitions is also relevant to curriculum planning. I suggested that the 'ideal' of the intercultural speaker is one which can be attained by learners and that it may be reasonable to conceive a 'threshold' at which learners become interculturally competent. This implies a minimal element of progression and raises the question whether a curriculum should use such a threshold as a point of orientation. The curriculum might be designed to ensure that the threshold is attainable, but it might also include elements which take learners beyond the threshold, although not necessarily in a linear or step-by-step fashion. The threshold is also a possible point of orientation for assessment and certification purposes.

A Threshold of Intercultural Communicative Competence?

The notion of a threshold in foreign language competence was introduced in the work of the Council of Europe team.[2] There the concept is closely related to the use of the native speaker as a model for the language learner:

> Until he has reached full native-like command of the foreign language, the learner, *qua* learner, may be regarded as always being on his way towards this full command. (van Ek, 1980: 95)

Until the native-like command is reached, it is argued, learners need to perform 'adequately' in communication situations they meet. 'Adequacy' is however difficult to define, since it involves social acceptance by native speakers, as well as differing degrees of precision in linguistic performance according to the demands of the role the learner has in a given situation.

Furthermore van Ek suggests that a level defined as adequate must also have 'pedagogical adequacy' i.e. the potential for further development towards the native speaker ideal. Consequently, van Ek argues that a definition of a threshold in terms of 'the minimum needs of the majority of foreign language learners' would be too high, take too long to reach for many learners and discourage beginners. He therefore proposes a threshold which is 'attainable in a relatively short period of time' (van Ek, 1980: 96) somewhere between the level of minimum needs — which he equates with the existing German *Volkshochschulzertifikat* — and zero-level. He mentions in passing that a second level would correspond to the *Volkshochschulzertifikat*, a level which has yet to be defined in detail, although a 'Vantage Level' is currently being elaborated (van Ek & Trim, 1996).

It is evident from this that the threshold level is determined in part by intuitions about learners' needs and pedagogical concerns about motivation. As Roulet points out, this produces some ambiguities with respect to determining needs:

> *Tout d'abord, rien ne permet d'affirmer que le niveau-seuil constitue un tronc commun, un passage minimal obligé pour tous les adultes apprenant une langue seconde; les situations de communication dans lesquelles peuvent se trouver des touristes et des travailleurs migrants sont si différents qu'il paraît difficile, ou du moins peu économique, de satisfaire les besoins langagiers des uns et des autres à l'aide d'un tronc commun (...) Selon le type de public visé, une sélection devra être opérée dans l'inventaire des actes de paroles et des notions, comme dans la liste de leurs réalisations linguistiques.* (1977: 4)[3]

A definition of a threshold level for ICC would differ from van Ek's approach in a number of ways. First, since the competence of the intercultural speaker is different from that of the native speaker, and is attainable by language learners, the notion of 'adequacy' as an interim and imperfect stage of learning is replaced by adequacy defined as the ability to function as an intercultural speaker. When the language learner has reached this stage, they need go no further. The question nonetheless arises as to whether they *can* go further and whether for certification purposes it is necessary to define more advanced stages.

van Ek's proposal to define adequacy also in terms of what is attainable in a relatively short period of time and therefore helpful in maintaining learner motivation, in fact leads to a threshold definition which is less than adequate for 'minimum needs of the majority of foreign language learners'. The concern about motivation and attainability is a pragmatic issue and context-dependent. In principle it should not affect a theoretical definition of a threshold for ICC. On the other hand, since the model proposed has educational objectives related to locations of learning in educational institutions, it is necessary to take account of the pragmatic issue for ICC too, i.e. of which objectives can be realised in a given situation.

Roulet's argument that the Threshold Level cannot be a common core but that there has to be selection of content for different learner groups, is related to my general argument that realisations of an abstract model must take account of the factors in particular circumstances. A threshold for ICC is therefore likely to differ from context to context in terms of which components are emphasised and which objectives are prioritised or even excluded from each component. The decision will be partly in terms of foreseeable needs and opportunities for intercultural communication and partly in terms of the cognitive and affective development of the learners.

In time, a threshold for ICC will be defined for each context and will not be an interim attainment, a stage on the way to a goal, but rather the goal itself, i.e. the ability to function as an intercultural speaker. The notion of stages on the way to a desirable goal is replaced by the notion that the goal may be more complex in some circumstances than others and therefore the demands on learners greater and more complex. This will depend for example on opportunities for face-to-face interaction, or on the emphasis given to each skill, or on what knowledge of another country and culture is thought to be necessary. In a given case, a learner can be deemed to perform adequately when they can perform to the satisfaction of all concerned — including themselves — in all the situations they actually meet. This pre-supposes that the prediction of what a learner is likely to meet has been accurate and those situations do not require competences or objectives within them which were excluded in the original definition for the particular learning context. This in turn implies that performance can be 'less than satisfactory' and 'more than satisfactory' and perhaps even more refinements of judgement can be devised, as an answer to the question whether it is necessary and possible to define different levels of attainment for purposes of certification. It is also important to bear in mind that 'performance' is used here to cover all the objectives of ICC, including those of knowledge (*savoirs*) and attitudes (*savoir être*) for example, which do not necessarily involve interaction with others.

I am aware that this proposal defining a threshold in ICC raises problems for traditional methods of assessment and I shall return to the issues in Chapter 5.

Planning a Curriculum for Intercultural Communicative Competence

Although I have argued that curricula must be planned for each context, I propose to set out the general processes involved as a consequence of the view of ICC taken here. I shall do so by suggesting a number of separate stages of analysis and decision-making, although some overlap is inevitable.

Stage 1 : The geo-political context

An analysis of what might be meant by ICC in the situation in question. If learners live in a situation where they have no foreseeable face-to-face interaction with native speakers of a language, their needs will be different from those who are in constant contact, as visitors or hosts, or those who mainly use the language as a lingua franca. This analysis has to draw upon a societal as well as an individual perspective; individual learners' foreseeable needs may differ from the general level of intercultural contact in a society as it currently exists and as its body politic perceives the future.

Stage 2 : The learning context

An analysis of the learning locations and other parameters. In some circumstances, the option of fieldwork may not exist or the opportunities for independent learning through the media may be limited. Since curricula are usually determined to some degree by bodies other than the teacher and learners, it is also necessary to analyse the parameters set by such bodies in order to see whether there are constraints imposed which contradict the objectives of ICC, for example by those responsible for certification.

Stage 3 : The developmental factor

An analysis of the cognitive and affective development of the learners. Although individual learners develop at different rates and in different ways, consideration must be given to this element in the teaching and learning. It need not be a constraint in that teachers may decide that exposure to certain kinds of learning experience in various locations can be successful despite the apparent lack of readiness of the learners involved. It may however be the case that the teacher decides that some objectives are inappropriate for their learners.

Stage 4 : Identification of objectives

The decision about which objectives should be set as the guidelines for the curriculum is made in the light of the preceding stages of analysis.

Objectives and further specifications as suggested in Chapter 3, for the skills, knowledge and attitudes for intercultural competence need to be complemented by similar objectives and specifications for linguistic, socio-linguistic and discourse competence.

Stage 5 : The ICC threshold

At this point it is useful to specify, as a summary of preceding stages, the threshold/goal of ICC for the learners involved. The definition should include reference to the following:

- the geo-political context: the present and foreseeable needs and uses of the particular language for learners of the country in question, described in terms of the country's political, commercial and other relevant relationships with countries where the language is spoken natively, and/or in terms of the use of the language as a lingua franca and the advantages which that might bring;
- the locations and parameters of the teaching and learning situation: the time available for learning and the methods and materials which might be included; the availability and nature of contact with other speakers of the language, native or not, and the cultures which they embody;
- the situations in which it is foreseen learners will draw upon their ICC: specimen examples of intercultural communication situations and of the competences needed, from a situation where learners have no personal contact with speakers of the language and do not need the skills of real time interaction, for example, to a situation where learners' daily requirements and experience depend on successful interaction with a constantly changing flow of other intercultural speakers of the language as lingua franca.

Stage 6 : Sequence in the curriculum

Ordering and prioritisation of objectives. Although I have argued against traditional conceptions of linear and cumulative progression, it is possible to prioritise the 'edges and corners' of the jigsaw and consider their relationship to the different locations and opportunities for learning. Since some objectives may have been excluded for a particular group of learners, each jigsaw will be different. After the frame has been prioritised, the choice of elements within the jigsaw can be made as a function of the interests of the learners, and it is at this point that consultation with learners is productive. The implication of this is of course that not all curriculum planning decisions can be taken in advance, and that some elements of the jigsaw will be in that part of the curriculum which is future as well as contemporary independent learning.

What I have called the 'edges and corners' needs further explanation. It refers to a combination of all components of ICC. There are established views on priorities in linguistic competence, although these are not inviolate. There are intuitive views on priorities in 'knowledge'. These priorities are also determined in part by consideration of learners' perceived needs and levels of psychological development. In some institutional settings it is also possible to take into consideration learners' experience in other subject areas, and the possibility of co-operation across the curriculum. There is much less existing consideration of priorities in the skills and attitudes dimensions of ICC.

Some attitudes can only develop in fieldwork or independent learning locations, for example 'the readiness to experience different stages of adaptation to and interaction with another culture during a period of residence'. There are also some skills which depend on the opportunity for real time interaction with an interlocutor from another culture. I have pointed out the significance of the developmental factor too. These considerations apart, skills and attitudes have to develop holistically in relation to the cultural and linguistic content of a proposed course, i.e. it is not appropriate to cut the relationships and links between the different components. The degree of difficulty in the skills and the maturity in attitudes will depend on the nature of the content and the teaching and learning techniques proposed. The priorities of linguistic competence and of knowledge will continue to be significant but be tempered by consideration of the need to develop attitudes and skills simultaneously. Finally, the notion of a 'spiral curriculum' provides a frame for revisiting and deepening familiarity with aspects of linguistic and knowledge content as well as skills and attitudes.

An Example: Teaching French in an East Coast Region of the USA

Stage 1 : The geo-political context

Pupils learning French in secondary education in this region live in a society which has limited direct connections with France or other francophone countries. There is no foreseeable societal need for substantial numbers of speakers of French as a foreign language. Even if trade with the European Union is a significant part of US policy, the use of English in Western Europe will allow access to all the member states, including France and Belgium. Furthermore, travel to francophone countries by individuals for business or leisure reasons is likely to be relatively insignificant and not sufficient justification in itself for teaching French. Finally, the numbers of native or heritage speakers of French in the USA are small and geographically distant from this region; again, this is an insufficient justification. The fundamental justification is described in the National Standards document:

> Even if students never speak the language after leaving school, for a lifetime they will retain the cross-cultural (*in our terminology: 'intercultural'*) skills and knowledge, the insight, and the access to a world beyond traditional borders. (*Standards for Foreign Language Learning*, 1996: 24)

Therefore intercultural *communicative* competence *in French* is not a long-term goal, even if it is used as a learning goal for the medium term, i.e. end of High School. The National Standards view suggests that intercultural competence transferable to encounters with otherness in later life is at least as important as linguistic competence.

Stage 2 : The learning context

Pupils begin to learn French in Grade 9, at age 13/14, and continue to do so for six years, although they may opt out at the end of any year. Their curriculum is/will be framed by a National Standards document which establishes 'what students should know and be able to do' by the end of High School. These recommendations are then realised in state and local curricula, and the teaching plans of the individual teacher. The National Standards document includes full recognition of the cultural dimension although the terminology of 'mastery' of a culture is suspect:

> Through the study of other languages students gain a knowledge and understanding of the cultures that use that language and, in fact, cannot truly master the language until they have also mastered the cultural contexts in which the language occurs. (Executive summary. *Standards for Foreign Language Learning: Preparing for the 21st Century*, 1996)

Pupils have five hours classroom instruction per week. Other opportunities for learning are very limited. The nearest location for fieldwork would be francophone Canada but in practice this is not normally included in the curriculum. There are however opportunities to watch television programmes from France by cable TV and there are substantial numbers of native speakers of French in the region, not least due to the international community in Washington DC. Finally there is some opportunity for help and support from the French Embassy. All this suggests that the principal learning location is the classroom and that there are some opportunities for independent learning in the immediate environment; a fieldwork location does not exist.

Stage 3 : The developmental factor

At age 13/14, it is probable that a group of pupils is very diverse in development, some ready to handle abstract concepts, others not, some more readily able to decentre and take another's perspective, others largely ethnocentric. Their existing knowledge of their own national culture is probably substantial, as they are well into their process of secondary socialisation, but will have significant, but not easily predictable gaps. Their knowledge of francophone countries will be superficial and perhaps stereotyped and prejudiced. Given the geo-political situation and lack of substantial connections with the francophone world, it is unlikely that pupils will have a particular interest in *la Francophonie*.

All this suggests that teachers can take little for granted, that in the early years particularly, learners need to work from concrete to abstract, that not all pupils will grasp abstract issues or abandon ethnocentric attitudes. In particular, insufficient knowledge and experience of francophone countries, and the stereotypes and prejudices which arise, suggest that particular attention must be paid to these.

Stage 4 : Identification of objectives

In a learning context where the predominant location is the classroom, some objectives are much less easily attained than others. The lack of opportunity for real time interaction with interlocutors from a francophone country or community means that the competences which include skills of interaction or negotiation can only be partially attained and are unlikely to be needed. These skills include: in sociolinguistic competence, negotiating or making explicit presupposed meanings; in discourse competence, negotiation of conventions for intercultural interaction and texts; and in intercultural competence, the skill of interaction and the skill of discovery insofar as it is dependent on elicitation from native speakers.

The competences and objectives which can be pursued and serve as end-of-course aims are:

- linguistic competence: the ability to apply knowledge of (some of) the rules of a standard version of the language to produce and interpret spoken and written language;
- (part of) sociolinguistic competence: the ability to give to language produced or interpreted, meanings which are taken for granted by interlocutors;

- (part of) discourse competence: the ability to use and discover strategies for the production and interpretation of monologue or dialogue texts which follow the conventions of the culture;
- (part of) intercultural competence (see descriptions in Chapter 3):
  - attitudes: objectives (a), (b), (c)
  - knowledge: objectives (a), (b), (c), (d), (e), (f), (g), (h), (i), (j), (k)
  - skills of interpreting and relating: objectives (a), (b)
  - skills of discovery and interaction: objectives (a), (b), (e)
  - critical cultural awareness: objectives (a), (b).

Given the minimal opportunities for interaction, much classroom work will be focused on documents provided for learners, complemented by opportunities to reflect upon and analyse their independent learning from the media.

Stage 5 : The ICC threshold

ICC for a pupil/student in this region of the USA will include attitudes of interest in otherness and willingness to question the assumptions of their own culture, comparing them with assumptions in the other. They will have a substantial knowledge of the culture of at least one francophone country and parallel phenomena in their own country. They will be able to observe, analyse and interpret documents or events in the other culture and in their own, drawing upon their existing knowledge to do so and able to discover further knowledge where necessary. They will be able to identify the value assumptions in such documents and events and make a judgement on them from an explicit perspective and explicit criteria. In order to analyse and interpret documents or events, they will draw upon their knowledge of and ability to use the standard language of the country in question. This will mean drawing upon their knowledge of the meanings and conventions most frequently associated, in that country, with the language and genres of the documents or events in question.

The situations in which learners will draw upon their ICC, once they have attained a threshold, will be of two kinds. First, they have many opportunities to encounter otherness within their own country, with its many diverse cultures. Although the diversity can be identified and is marked by use of different varieties of language, these are often difficult to perceive for the non-specialist, and the competences upon which they will draw most frequently are the intercultural and the sociolinguistic, rather than linguistic and discourse competences. They will be interested in and able to interpret and relate to the emblems, values and meanings of otherness within their own country.

A second kind of encounter is with otherness of foreign countries. Here too, the opportunity to use their linguistic competence is likely to be infrequent, but their awareness of the interdependence of language and cultural meanings — their understanding that another language is not simply an encoding of their own language and meanings — will be a significant contribution to their readiness to take a different perspective and to expect that speakers of other languages will have different conceptualisations of (parts of) their shared reality. They will also be aware that non-native speakers of English will use it in a different way to themselves, and that they will need to take account of this in English-medium interaction.

Stage 6 : Sequence in the curriculum

Given the age and development of the pupils, one priority in establishing the 'edges and corners' should be a juxtapositioning of francophone and American cultures (knowledge objective (a)). Taking into consideration other work across the curriculum it is also possible to prioritise 'geographical space' in the two countries (knowledge objectives (f) and (g)). Neither of these would be treated exhaustively, neither at this point nor in the future, but would be revisited in accordance with a 'spiral curriculum'.

The issue of priorities in linguistic competence would be met by the selection of documents, authentic and contrived, which reflect the rules of the standard language, and the sociolinguistically determined meanings in the documents. These might involve generalised and stereotyping statements by, for example, a French native speaker on the geography and regional identities of the USA, and a parallel document from an American perspective on France, presented in accessible language. The documents should be conceived in such a way as to allow easy analysis of ethnocentric perspectives and values in order to begin the development of skills of interpreting and relating, together with the identification of values, with a view to developing a critical framework over time. (A possible theme for the study of 'national memory' in France and the USA would be the sale of territory by Napoleon to the US government.)

The knowledge objectives for medium-term treatment would be those focusing on the processes of misunderstanding and dysfunction and those concerned with the means of achieving contact with interlocutors from another country (objectives (c) and (b)). The lack of significance of contacts at a geo-political level and of the possibilities of real time contact locally mean that these objectives will only become meaningful to learners when they have acquired some knowledge and developed attitudes of interest in otherness.

The attitude objectives identified as relevant here cannot be prioritised. On the other hand they must be considered in the context of psychological, particularly moral, development. The inclusion of teaching documents which have ethnocentric attitudes inherent in them and which are subject to analysis, provides ethnocentric learners with a familiar perspective on others but also subjects that perspective — and by implication their own — to a critique. Provided the critique is not aggressive and, for example, the documents chosen demonstrate the benefits of suspending one's ethnocentric perceptions, the classroom process may help to initiate development of understanding in individual learners.

Notes

1. Other uses of the term 'curriculum' are more inclusive than this, and refer to teaching methods, learning styles, implicit and explicit values — the 'hidden curriculum' — but I shall use the term only to include objectives and a description of what needs to be learnt to attain them.
2. Cummins (1984) also uses the term to describe levels of competence in bilingual children which enables them to benefit from academic work in their languages. This is a related issue but has not, to my knowledge, been directly compared.
3. First of all, it is not possible to state that the threshold level constitutes a common core, a minimum which is obligatory for all adults learning a second language; the communication situations in which tourists and migrant workers find themselves are so different that it is difficult, or at least hardly economical, to satisfy the language needs of both by a common core (...) A selection must be made, according to the clientele envisaged, from the inventory of speech acts and notions, and from the list of their linguistic realisations.

Chapter 5

Assessment

Introduction

One of the main arguments in this monograph has been that foreign language teaching is a social phenomenon which is in part determined by the nature of the particular context in which it takes place. In Chapter 1, I described a number of cases in order to show their relationship to the configuration of circumstances and the effect on the determination of aims for FLT. At the same time, it has been my purpose to discuss intercultural communicative competence in such a way that the discussion is of value in any situation. More specifically, in Chapters 2 and 3, I attempted to define and describe ICC in a comprehensive way whilst being aware that in some situations something less than comprehensive ICC would be an appropriate aim for FLT. This was all the more evident in Chapter 4, when I suggested that the selection of objectives for learners from a comprehensive model would be the first step in the design of an appropriate curriculum for a specific situation. The selection would be a function of the social and geo-political factors in the learners' environment.

This basic issue is equally important with respect to assessment. It is, first of all, self-evident that a selection of objectives from the comprehensive description of ICC means that assessment should focus on those objectives only, i.e. on determining in how far learners have reached the competence described by those selected objectives. There is a second, related issue: the purposes of assessment are also determined by context. The context includes the educational institution and the societal and geo-political factors to which educational institutions and the education system as a whole must respond. This is most evident with respect to certification, whereby the education system opens opportunities for individuals and also helps societies, as represented by their governments, to plan for predicted needs in the workforce. As societies change, increasingly in the contemporary world in response to forces at inter-societal levels, the predicted needs also change, and lead to changes in certification. Existing certificates may be altered to emphasise different purposes, with a consequent effect on curricula, and new certificates and curricula are developed to accommodate the ambitions of individuals and the predictions of governments.

On the other hand, education systems are not only reactive but also pro-active. They have their internal dynamic, for example with respect to their views on how best to reach the goals set for them, how the objectives should be formulated, or how best to organise certification. New methods of teaching and learning arise mainly from within the education profession, as do new approaches to assessment. In particular, the hope that teaching, learning and assessment — and therefore also certification — can be treated holistically, has led to a reappraisal of assessment. Gipps (1994: 167) argues that what is needed is a 'paradigm shift':

> Assessment is not an exact science, and we must stop presenting it as such. This is of course part of the post-modern condition — a suspension of belief in the absolute status of 'scientific' knowledge.

She describes this as a 'shift from a psychometric model of assessment to an educational model', and argues that 'educational assessment' is characterised by its potential for enhancing good quality learning. What is needed are assessment programmes which have a positive impact on teaching and learning (ibid.: 158). This position will be fundamental to my discussion of the assessment of ICC, and I shall rely to a considerable extent on Gipps' analysis.

The purpose of this chapter is to consider, at a level of principle, what might be appropriate ways of assessing those dimensions of ICC which have been the focus of earlier chapters: knowledge (*savoirs*), skills (*savoir comprendre, savoir apprendre/faire*), attitudes (*savoir être*) and critical cultural awareness (*savoir s'engager*). This will be done on the continuing assumption that FLT takes place in educational institutions and has educational objectives (political education), and it is for that reason that Gipps' argument for educational assessment is important here. Secondly, I shall continue to assume a model of ICC which includes linguistic, sociolinguistic and discourse competences, a model which is holistic and analysed into its components only in order to develop a better understanding of what is essentially one competence. The analysis of components allows us to determine more precisely what our teaching aims should be, as I argued in earlier chapters, and also if and how we can assess the different dimensions of ICC separately or as a whole. I shall not focus in detail however on the assessment of linguistic, sociolinguistic or discourse competence, except with respect to the links and relationships with other competences.

Assessing the Five '*savoirs*'

As a first stage in the discussion of assessment I propose to put in abeyance the question of whether ICC should be assessed holistically. The identification of five *savoirs* allowed me to define them in terms of objectives and further specifications for teaching and curriculum planning and I propose to use this as a basis for discussing the assessment of learners' achievement with respect to those objectives. I shall return to the issues of holistic or separate assessment and related questions of validity and reliability in a later section. Here I shall take the objectives and specifications from Chapters 2 and 3 and discuss the implications for assessment.

Throughout my discussion I have used the term 'competence' and as we come to issues of assessment, it is important to focus on the implications of the term. It was introduced in order to maintain links with existing conceptions of FLT. Such links are important in ensuring that proposals for change in concepts and practice are understood, and considered by FLT professionals to be feasible. Nonetheless it is evident that terminology carries within it views which need to be made explicit. First, there is the relationship of competence to performance and the related question of 'performance assessment' as opposed to psychometric, 'objective' testing. Since the five *savoirs* include attitudes (*savoir être*) dispositions or orientations to act (*savoir s'engager), knowledge (savoirs*) and skills (*savoir comprendre, apprendre, faire*), it is evident that the distinction of competence and performance introduced by Chomsky and developed by Hymes is not adequate. It is here that the advantage of using the term '*savoir*' holistically becomes clear, since it includes the whole range of skills, attitudes and knowledge, and simultaneously allows us to distinguish among them by adding a second infinitive.[1]

Secondly, as stated in Chapter 2, the 'objectives' defined for each *savoir* are not restricted to those which are observable as behaviour or changes in behaviour. This was done in order to develop a more complex and comprehensive definition. As a consequence, performance assessment cannot be the only approach if all aspects of the five *savoirs* are to be assessed, since performance assessment relies on what is observable:

> there is agreement in the educational assessment profession that: 'Performance measurement calls for examinees to demonstrate their capabilities directly, by creating some product or engaging in some activity' (Haertel, 1992) and that there is heavy reliance on observation and/or professional judgement in the evaluation of the response (Mehrens, 1992) including teacher-examiners grading coursework and marking essay scripts. (Gipps, 1994: 99)

It might be argued that assessment for certification has to be restricted to performance assessment as defined here, omitting any aspect of the five *savoirs* which is not observable. I shall consider this later but initially ignore that constraint in order to explore all the possibilities.

Another interpretation of a competence/performance distinction is to identify the former with underlying understanding, metacognition, and the ability to reflect on one's own thinking and response to experience. Entwistle (cited in Gipps, 1994) makes a distinctions between 'deep learning' and 'shallow learning', the former being characterised as:

- an intention to understand material for oneself;
- interacting vigorously and critically with the content;
- relating ideas to previous knowledge and experience;
- using organising principles to integrate ideas;
- relating evidence to conclusions; and
- examining the logic of the argument. (Gipps, 1994: 24)

In order to achieve many of the objectives of the five *savoirs*, such learning is a *sine qua non*. For example, *savoir apprendre* involves relating new information to existing knowledge; *savoir comprendre* requires the use of organising principles to relate conflicting interpretations of phenomena; *savoir s'engager* involves interacting vigorously and critically with knowledge and experience. One of Gipps' main arguments is that such learning cannot be assessed, or encouraged, by psychometric objective testing, and it is clear that her argument is eminently applicable to ICC. The specifications of the five *savoirs* in Chapter 3 cannot, in most cases, be tested by multiple choice questions. The evidence for judging whether a learner has achieved objectives related to 'deep learning' has to be interpreted. If the interpretation of evidence is itself to be open to scrutiny, for example by the learner or by agencies outside an education system, it has to be based on explicit and agreed criteria.

A step towards the development of criteria for judgement was made in Chapter 3 when I suggested for each objective what might 'count as' a specification of that objective. In the first instance these further specifications can be used to decide on curricula, as in Chapter 4, but they can also be a starting point for deciding on criteria for assessment. For example, in *savoirs*, the specification of the first objective indicates the significance of 'events', 'individuals' and 'diverse interpretations of events' with respect to knowledge about 'historical and contemporary relationships':

> The intercultural speaker: knows about events, significant individuals and diverse interpretations of events which have involved both countries, and the traces left in the national memory, and about political and economic factors in the contemporary alliances of each country.

In order to develop assessment criteria from this, it would be necessary to decide whether knowledge of a 'given list' of events and individuals is required, or whether learners should know of some examples and be able to explain what they exemplify. In the latter case, assessors would also have evidence of 'deep learning', whereas the former case might only draw upon 'shallow learning' of information and knowledge of historical relationships, acquired without a fundamental understanding of the issues and principles involved. In both cases, the question of whether the learning has been adequate has to be addressed too, and this cannot be divorced from the discussion of progression and a 'threshold' raised in Chapter 4, to which I shall return in a later section of this current chapter.

This example from *savoirs* lies within familiar frameworks for assessment. More complex and novel issues arise with respect to other *savoirs*, notably *savoir être*, and I propose, as a next stage in the discussion, to work through the five *savoirs* in order to show how assessment can be applied, in different ways, to all of them.

I begin with 'attitudes' and the first objective:

Attitudes (savoir être)*: curiosity and openness, readiness to suspend disbelief about other cultures and belief about one's own.*

Objective (a):

(a) willingness to seek out or take up opportunities to engage with otherness in a relationship of equality, distinct from seeking out the exotic or to profit from others.

> The intercultural speaker is interested in the other's experience of daily life in contexts not usually presented to outsiders through the media or used to develop a commercial relationship with outsiders; is interested in the daily experience of a range of social groups within a society and not only that represented in the dominant culture.

In order to develop assessment criteria for this objective, it is necessary to ask what would count as evidence for interest in 'daily experience' or for interest in 'a range of social groups', rather than that which is the focus of commercial or media relationships with another society. One kind of evidence would be an expression of preference for 'daily experience' and an interest in other than dominant social groups.

An *expression* of preference would have to be more than an attitude — 'if I had a choice, I would ...' — and might be elicited by asking learners to make and explain a choice as part of assessed performance. For example learners might be asked to choose between two representations of an aspect of a foreign culture in order to use the representation — a text, an image, an audio or video-recording — as a basis for explaining the other culture to an interlocutor from their own culture. The choice of text would be evidence of their focus of interest. The way in which they then use the chosen text would be the basis for assessing other objectives.

Objective (b):

(b) interest in discovering other perspectives on interpretation of familiar and unfamiliar phenomena both in one's own and in other cultures and cultural practices.

> The intercultural speaker does not assume that familiar phenomena — cultural practices or products common to themselves and the other — are understood in the same way, or that unfamiliar phenomena can only be understood by assimilating them to their own cultural phenomena, that they need to discover the other's understanding of these, and of phenomena in their own culture which are not familiar to the other.

Criteria on which to judge learners' interest in other perspectives would need evidence of their not prioritising their own over other perspectives, of their choosing the other's explanation of phenomena in the learner's own culture. As with objective (a), this evidence would have to be action demonstrating preference, rather than a statement about preference. In objective (b), it would be important not to formulate preference in terms of evaluative comparison — 'the other's perspective is better than mine' — but to ensure that there is preference for an explanation which is a better fit to the perspective of the other. The preference in objective (a) is also a decision about what is more suitable for the purpose of explaining an aspect of another culture, a better fit.

Objective (c):

(c) willingness to question the values and presuppositions in cultural practices and products in one's own environment.

> The intercultural speaker actively seeks the other's perspectives and evaluations of phenomena in the speaker's environment which are taken for granted, and takes up the other's perspectives in order to contrast and compare with the dominant evaluations in their own society.

Evidence for learners' willingness to question the values of their own cultural environment might involve their choosing the other's interpretations and evaluations of phenomena which are fundamental to the learners' society and rarely questioned within it. Again this would be a performance rather than an attitude.

These first three objectives are related. In practice it would probably be necessary to evaluate them together, as three aspects of *savoir être*. It would also be possible to obtain evidence from the same performance for learners' *savoirs* and their *savoir comprendre*. Indeed, if the view is taken that ICC must be assessed holistically, then it would be important to invent a method of assessment which produces evidence for some or all of the five *savoirs* simultaneously. This is based on the assumption that the assessment will be undertaken at one point in time by an assessor not otherwise involved with the learner.

There are two other approaches. First, it is possible to assess over a period rather than at one given point in time. Evidence can therefore be identified as it arises in the course of learning, and need not be multi-purpose. This is possible for example when the assessor is also the teacher and in contact with the learner frequently. Second, it is also possible for learners to be their own assessors and this too allows for other modes of collecting evidence. The learner could for example assemble evidence in a portfolio. It is noteworthy that a learner able to do this would need a high degree of self-awareness and ability to reflect on their own actions. This is of the same nature as the defining characteristics of 'deep learning', i.e. an ability to relate (their own) actions and ideas to principles and to the abstract definitions of objectives such as those offered here.

Objective (d):

(d) readiness to experience the different stages of adaptation to and interaction with another culture during a period of residence.

> The intercultural speaker is able to cope with different kinds of experience of otherness (e.g. enthusiasm, withdrawal) during residence, and place them in a longer period of phases of acceptance and rejection.

Evidence for this objective will not be directly observable to an external assessor, since the objective describes the individual's ability to reflect on their experience and affective responses and to analyse them in terms of a framework of ideas on 'culture shock' (e.g. Furnham & Bochner, 1986). This requires a high degree of self-awareness, the ability to analyse one's own feelings of enthusiasm or of dismay, and to see them as part of a developmental reaction to otherness. The analysis may take place simultaneously ('I know I am experiencing culture shock and this phase will pass') or retrospectively ('I remember that I thought everything was perfect at the beginning'). The stimulus for this self-analysis can come from within the learner, particularly if they have had previous experience of culture shock. It can also come from another person, a teacher or mentor who urges the learner to reflect on their affective responses by referring them to a framework of ideas on culture shock. In both cases the evidence comes from the learner's reflections, rather than from a closely structured assessment instrument. The evidence is also likely to appear at a number of different points in the experience, and this suggests it needs to be collected over time, for example as part of a portfolio.

Objective (e):

(e) readiness to engage with the conventions and rites of verbal and non-verbal communication and interaction.

> The intercultural speaker notes and adopts the behaviours specific to a social group in a way in which they and the members of that group consider to be appropriate for an outsider; the intercultural speaker thus takes into consideration the expectations members of the group may have about appropriate behaviour for foreigners.

What is at issue here is the fact that native speakers do not necessarily accept that intercultural speakers should adopt and imitate the conventions of interaction (particularly those which are non-verbal) which are the norm for their group. The intercultural speaker too may not wish to adopt conventions which engage their whole personality and cultural identity, again particularly the non-verbal conventions which are often unconscious. They may be able to accept intellectually that a particular gesture is a norm of greeting, but resist doing it themselves because it is very different from their own non-verbal behaviour. For example, the convention of men greeting each other by kissing on both cheeks is, for members of some cultures, breaking a taboo on male–male physical contact. Such taboos are difficult to overcome because they are part of early socialisation. The ability of a successful intercultural speaker is to find a *modus vivendi* satisfactory to themselves and their interlocutors.[2] As with objective (d), the evidence for this objective is likely to appear over time, to be provided by learners themselves as they reflect on and analyse the process of finding a *modus vivendi*, and therefore become part of a portfolio. Table 5.1 summarises modes of assessment for attitudes.

Knowledge (savoirs)*: of social groups and their products and practices in one's own and in one's interlocutor's country, and of the general processes of societal and individual interaction.*

The assessment of knowledge in the sense of 'know that' (Ryle, 1949) is familiar ground but, as suggested earlier, the distinction between deep and

Table 5.1 Summary of modes of assessment for attitudes

Objective	*Kind of evidence*	*Where*
Attitudes (*savoir être*)		
(a) 'equality'	choice of representations of 'daily life'	test and/or portfolio
(b) 'other perspectives'	choice of analysis from a 'better fit' perspective	test and/or portfolio
(c) 'question own values'	choice of other evaluations of phenomena in own society	test and/or portfolio
(d) 'culture shock'	self-analysis, simultaneous or retrospective, of affective responses at different points	portfolio
(e) 'conventions of interaction'	self-analysis of processes of adaptation	portfolio

shallow learning adds a fresh perception and implies that techniques are also needed to assess deep learning as well as learners' ability to reiterate facts. This is however not new ground, since such traditional methods of assessment as essay-writing seek to explore the ability to use ideas in new situations, to relate factual knowledge to argument, to draw upon logical relationships within frameworks of knowledge, to interpret and come to sound conclusions.

An analysis of examinations at the end of upper secondary education in England (Byram, Morgan *et al.*, 1994: 140–145) reveals that essays written in French on aspects of French culture are marked under four main categories: understanding the question and providing relevant answers; structuring and organising the essay competently; displaying a breadth of knowledge; and demonstrating analytical skills and understanding. The second and last in this list are attempts to identify deep learning, and considerable emphasis is given to these categories. In fact, our criticism of these examinations is that too little attention is paid to the assessment of cultural knowledge and too much to these other factors, which can also be found in assessment of learners' knowledge of other subjects. The potential problem of reliability in assessing for example 'analytical skills' and understanding could be handled by formulating explicit and detailed criteria. It is then usual practice to provide a number of exemplars for the criteria, together with the training of assessors to ensure that they operate the criteria in the same way. In the case of the English examinations, detailed criteria do not exist. Professional judgement, formed on the basis of implicit criteria, and supported by double marking and discussion of critical cases, is considered reliable.[3] The process is time-consuming but is accepted as necessary to guarantee the quality of assessment for what is considered by many people to be the most important examination in the education system.

There are three inter-related categories of *savoirs* included in the definition of the knowledge objective: about aspects of a foreign culture; about one's own culture; about relationships between cultures at societal and individual level. The latter depends on the other two. Learners need to understand how aspects of one culture are perceived from another cultural perspective and how this link between two cultures is fundamental to interaction and communication. If assessment of *savoirs* is to take this into consideration, then techniques which reveal deep learning are essential. At intermediate and advanced level, the essay or similar approach can be appropriate. At a beginners' level, learners can be asked to comment on and explain illustrations of specific objectives. At all levels, learners can also be assessed on their factual knowledge and this can include 'objective' questions.

Let us take two examples, one focused on knowledge about the two cultures and the second focused on relationships.

Objective (h):

(h) knowledge about the processes and institutions of socialisation in one's own and one's interlocutor's country.

> The intercultural speaker knows about education systems, religious institutions, and similar locations where individuals acquire a national identity, are introduced to the dominant culture in their society, pass through specific rites marking stages in the life-cycle, in both their own and the other country.

A beginning learner of German might have been introduced, under this objective, to the tradition of *Konfirmation* in Protestant Germany with the information that most young people go through this ceremony, whether they normally attend church or not. At intermediate and advanced levels, further knowledge would be acquired about practices in Catholic parts of Germany, about practices in the former German Democratic Republic, about statistical analyses of young people's attendance at church, about rites of passage for young Germans of Turkish origin. The quantity of knowledge would depend on the length of the course as well as the age and learning level of the students.

At all levels, learners' factual knowledge can be assessed as a function of what they have had opportunity to learn during the course. It is also possible that they have acquired further knowledge from other sources and a decision has to be made whether such knowledge is given credit. The decision will depend on the function of the assessment, whether it is to evaluate achievement during the course or whether it is to record learners' proficiency at a given point in time, in order for example to take up a particular post. The techniques could be question and answer, or might include a stimulus such as a photograph of young people in their *Konfirmation* dress and an invitation to comment and explain.

In the second technique it is to be expected that learners will also demonstrate their ability to relate *Konfirmation* to a framework of knowledge about the role of the church in Germany, to their knowledge of rites of passage and the role of the church in their own country. They might also be invited to comment critically on rites of passage as such, and draw upon their critical cultural awareness. As is often the case, a single technique can provide evidence for more than one *savoir*.

Objective (c):

(c) knowledge of the types of cause and process of misunderstanding between interlocutors of different cultural origins.

> The intercultural speaker knows about conventions of communication and interaction in their own and the foreign cultures, the unconscious effect of paralinguistic and non-verbal phenomena, alternative interpretations of shared concepts, gestures, customs and rituals.

Knowledge about intercultural communicative breakdown can be formulated in abstract terms, drawing upon interaction theory, but is more likely to be taught through examples. A learner of French might be taught to analyse conversation transcripts demonstrating conventions of turn-taking. An assessment exercise could involve analysis of comments by two individuals describing their feeling of discomfort in a conversation where one feels constantly 'cut off' and the other feels that their interlocutor is 'slow to respond'. The learner would need to refer to their knowledge of turn-taking in certain uses of French and in equivalent situations in their own country. This could also be linked with a text in which apparently similar concepts, which in fact have different significances, are the cause of misunderstanding. A parallel example to *Konfirmation* would be for an English learner of French to refer to '*la première communion*', and misunderstand it as 'first communion', the former being a widely accepted rite of passage irrespective of religious belief, the latter being confined to a minority of young people who attend church regularly. The ability to explain this misunderstanding would require reference to factual knowledge but also demonstrate the learner's capacity to draw upon a general framework of knowledge about socialisation practices to explain a specific instance. Table 5.2 summarises the modes of assessment for knowledge.

Table 5.2 Summary of modes of assessment for knowledge

Objective	*Kind of evidence*	*Where*
Knowledge (*savoirs*)	[same for all aspects (a) to (j)]	[same for all aspects (a) to (j)]
(a) historical and contemporary relationships (d & e) national memories (f & g) definitions of geographical space (h) socialisation (i) social distinctions (j) institutions	(i) factual knowledge elicited by question and answer; (ii) deep learning knowledge elicited by techniques requiring comment and analysis	(i) test (ii) continuous assessment (not self assessment)

Skills of interpreting and relating (savoir comprendre)*: ability to interpret a document or event from another culture, to explain it and relate it to documents or events from one's own.*

Since the skills of interpreting and relating are dependent upon knowledge, it will be evident that assessment is also inter-related. In fact, in suggesting that knowledge can be assessed through techniques which collect evidence of deep learning, I have already introduced the skills of interpreting and relating, by requiring 'comment' and 'analysis'. An additional dimension is included in objective (c).

Objective (c):

(c) ability to mediate between conflicting interpretations of phenomena.

> The intercultural speaker can use their explanations of sources of misunderstanding and dysfunction to help interlocutors overcome conflicting perspectives; can explain the perspective of each in terms accessible to the other; can help interlocutors to identify common ground and unresolvable difference.

This skill could be used in the written mode, when the intercultural speaker is a translator for example, who would provide a commentary where they see potential misunderstanding or dysfunction. This reduces the pressures of real-time interaction, allowing time for analysis and reference to existing knowledge or the use of skills of discovery (*savoir apprendre*) to acquire more knowledge. It is however likely that mediation will often take place in real-time interaction, with all the constraints and demands that this places on the intercultural speaker. The assessment of this skill can therefore be discussed in combination with the assessment of *savoir faire*.

Skills of discovery and interaction (savoir apprendre/faire)*: ability to acquire new knowledge of a culture and cultural practices, and the ability to operate* *knowledge, attitudes and skills under the constraints of real-time communication and interaction.*

Skills of discovery (*savoir apprendre*) have a pivotal place in my model of ICC. They allow the learner to escape the constraints of what can be learnt in the classroom. They are the means whereby skills of interpreting and relating can be supplemented when the learner meets unknown material. They are also connected with skills of interaction (*savoir faire*), since much though not all discovery is effected through interaction with native speakers. Discovery takes place in many instances in real-time and depends on the ability to ask the kinds of questions which elicit further knowledge especially when the interlocutor is unable to explain what is self-evident for them in their taken-for-granted reality. This is the significance of objective (a).

Objective (a):

(a) ability to elicit from an interlocutor the concepts and values of documents or events and to develop an exploratory system susceptible of application to other phenomena.

> The intercultural speaker can use a range of questioning techniques to elicit from informants the allusions, connotations and presuppositions of a document or event, and can develop and test generalisations about shared meaning and values (by using them to interpret another document; by questioning another informant; by consulting appropriate literature) and establish links and relationships among them (logical relationship of hierarchy, of cause and effect, of conditions and consequence, etc.)

Objective (b):

(b) ability to identify significant references within and across cultures and elicit their significance and connotations.

> The intercultural speaker can 'read' a document or event for the implicit references to shared meanings and values (of national memory, of concepts of space, of social distinction, etc.) particular to the culture of their interlocutor or of international currency (arising for example from the dominance of western satellite television); in the latter case, the intercultural speaker can identify or elicit different interpretations and connotations and establish relationships of similarity and difference between them.

The assessment of this skill is difficult. In one experiment (Byram, Morgan *et al.*, 1994: 163-165) students prepared and carried out an interview with a native speaker in order to explore the concept of regional identity. The interviewees were asked about how and to what extent they felt their social identity was related to their place of origin, e.g. what it means to say '*Je suis breton/alsacien...*'. This could be combined with a discussion with the assessor in which the student is invited to reflect on their findings, explain their approach and questioning technique, and suggest what generalisations they could hypothesise and how they would test them. For intermediate students this proved to be a difficult but productive task, requiring considerable linguistic, sociolinguistic and discourse competence. Advanced language learners trained in ethnographic data-collection skills can be highly successful in eliciting many kinds of data (Barro *et al.*, in press) and the possibility of assessing their skills from an audio-recording of an interview, combined with a discussion, would be worth further consideration.

Another objective and specification focuses on the use of skills of discovery where a native speaker interlocutor is not essential and where knowledge can be found in other sources too:

Objective (e):

(e) the ability to identify contemporary and past relationships between one's own and the other culture and society.

> The intercultural speaker can use sources (e.g. reference books, newspapers, histories, experts, lay informants) to understand political, economic and social relationships between cultures and societies, and analyse the differing interpretations involved.

It is possible to envisage a simulation where learners are provided with sources and asked to compare and analyse documents from their own and the other society. It is however also possible for evidence for this skill to be collected over time by learners and their teachers, for inclusion in a portfolio for example. Similarly objectives (a) and (b) need not be assessed in a test situation, but can be achieved in fieldwork or in coursework in the classroom. This approach to assessment, it is important to note, requires a high degree of self-awareness and understanding of the abstract principles underlying the use of skills of discovery. If learners are to select evidence appropriately, they need to be able to relate particular instances to general principles, and this suggests a capacity for abstract thinking which is often only developed in post-adolescence. Where learners have not acquired this degree of reflection, teachers can select evidence on their behalf.

The main characteristic of skills of interaction (*savoir faire*) is their operation in real time. They involve the operationalisation of the other components of ICC and integrate them in highly complex ways. Evidence of success in interaction is unlikely to be available directly, precisely because it takes place in real time and usually in circumstances which do not allow data collection. Indirect evidence can be provided *post hoc* by learners themselves or by others involved or able to observe. The learner who is able to negotiate agreement on conventions of interaction for a specific occasion (objective (c)), or to act in accordance with the degree of proximity to another language and culture (objective (d)), or use institutions to maintain contacts in another culture (objective (f)), or mediate between interlocutors from their own and another culture (objective (g)), would be able to reflect on and document the occasions, identifying in retrospect the issues and problems involved and the indicators of success. Table 5.3 summarises the modes of assessment for skills.

Critical cultural awareness (savoir s'engager)*: an ability to evaluate, critically and on the basis of explicit criteria, perspectives, practices and products in one's own and other cultures and countries.*

This 'educational' component of ICC adds the notion of evaluation and comparison not just for purposes of improving the effectiveness of communication and interaction but especially for purposes of clarifying one's own ideological perspective and engaging with others consciously on the basis of that perspective. The consequence may include conflict in perspectives, not only harmonious communication.

As with the other components there is some degree of overlap, so that skills of interpreting and discovery are linked to the first objective (a).

Objective (a):

(a) the ability to identify and interpret explicit or implicit values in documents and events in one's own and other cultures.

Similarly objectives (b) and (c) are related to skills of interpreting, relating and interaction but add the evaluative dimension.

Objective (b):

(b) the ability to make an evaluative analysis of the documents and events which refers to an explicit perspective and criteria.

Objective (c):

(c) the ability to interact and mediate in intercultural exchanges in accordance with explicit criteria, negotiating where necessary a degree of acceptance of those exchanges by drawing upon one's knowledge, skills and attitudes.

It will be evident that the opportunities for and constraints on assessment are similar to those for other components. The analysis and evaluation of

Table 5.3 Summary of modes of assessment for skills

Objective	*Kind of evidence*	*Where*
(i) Interpreting and relating (*savoir comprendre*)		
(a) identify ethnocentric perspectives	part of evidence from assessment of *savoirs* [above]	test and/or continuous assessment as for assessment of *savoirs*
(b) identify misunderstanding and dysfunction	ditto	ditto
(c) mediate between interpretations	part of assessment of interaction (see below)	
(ii) Discovery and interaction (*savoir apprendre/faire*)		
(a) questioning a native speaker	use of interviewing techniques	test simulation
(b) identify significant reference	ditto	portfolio
(e) use sources to understand relationships	use of reference books etc. to illuminate specific documents	test and/or coursework
(c) agree conventions	retrospective analysis and documentation by self and others	portfolio
(d) respond to distance/proximity of other culture	ditto	ditto
(f) institutions for contacts	ditto	ditto
(g) mediate between interlocutors	ditto	ditto

documents and events can be through testing which asks for commentary and analysis, whereas objective (c) takes place in real-time and is a particular version of the skills of interaction for which there can be only indirect evidence. Table 5.4 summarises the modes of assessment for critical cultural awareness.

In the above proposals for modes and locations of assessment, there is included in all but the assessment of *savoirs* the option of self-assessment to complement assessment by a teacher or tester. Self-assessment presupposes a high degree of self-awareness, the ability to reflect on one's own learning and achievement, which suggests in turn a particular mode of learning and

Table 5.4 Summary of modes of assessment for critical cultural awareness

Objective	*Kind of evidence*	*Where*
Critical cultural awareness (*savoir s'engager*)		
(a) identify values	part of evidence from assessment of *savoirs* and *savoir comprendre* (see above)	(see *savoirs* and *savoir comprendre*, above)
(b) evaluate by criteria	ditto	ditto
(c) interact and mediate	part of evidence of *savoir faire* (see above)	(see *savoir faire*, above)

teaching. The theory of experiential learning (Kolb, 1984) which argues that there is a need for alternation between engagement and reflection as discussed in Chapter 3, and the increasing attention to giving learners autonomy and control over their learning through developing their understanding of the processes of learning, their metacognition (Gipps, 1994: 24), are both sources to guide teaching. As well as facilitating the acquisition of skills, knowledge and attitudes, teaching can include reflection on what these consist of in more abstract terms. This will enhance the transferability of skills and attitudes so that learners have a generalisable critical cultural awareness as a basis for study of other cultures and languages or for coping with interaction in other cultural and linguistic environments.

If these metacognitive capacities for self-analysis are to be recognised in assessment, neither the testing of knowledge nor the evaluation of observable performance are sufficient. It is in the self-analytical and often retrospective accounts by a learner of their interaction, their *savoir faire* and *savoir s'engager*, that the main evidence will be found.

However, such evidence is not part of the traditions of assessment and may not be admissible in all circumstances. In order to refine the discussion, we need to consider the variety of purposes and circumstances for which assessment is needed.

Purposes for Assessment

Following Gipps (1994), I begin the discussion of the purposes in the assessment of ICC in terms of the contrast between assessment for accountability and educational assessment. Gipps writes from an Anglo-American perspective where there has been in recent years strong societal pressure to hold educational institutions accountable for the quality of the education they are providing and the finance which they need to do so. Accountability is sought through quantifiable evidence of learners' abilities gained in schools and universities. Moreover, in Britain, the introduction of comparisons between institutions on the basis of qualifications obtained by their students has given these an increased importance. In these circumstances, the question of reliability is particularly significant and there is a tendency to seek modes of assessment which break knowledge and abilities into closely defined and observable sub-sets. These can then be related to the teaching process, by asking whether what has been taught has in fact been learnt by students. Secondly, they can be assessed separately and with high reliability. 'Input' can be related to quantifiable and objectively observable 'output'.

This approach carries a number of presuppositions and implications. First, it assumes a 'transmission' view of teaching, i.e. that knowledge and abilities can be identified, isolated and transferred to the learner. Second, what is to be transmitted, can be put into an order of difficulty and learners acquire knowledge and abilities in that order, 'progressing' in a linear fashion. Third, the progress can be measured on a linear scale and the individual's progress can be reported in terms of comparison with what would be expected of any cross-section group from the general population to which the individual belongs. In other words, the assessment is norm-referenced. Fourth, such assessment usually takes place at the end of a course of learning, often corresponding to a point of transfer in the education system when students leave an institution to go to employment or move to another educational institution. In this case students' achievement is certificated on the basis of assessment and the certificate is a passport to new opportunities for employment or study, but also a passport which is recognised by some institutions and not others. The importance of the certificate for the individual reinforces the need for reliable assessment and objective testing of component parts of their knowledge and abilities.

In language testing this general approach has been realised as assessment of each defined skill separately from others. The techniques used have been chosen for their reliability as well as their validity, particularly the possibility of marking students' work without variation from one assessor to another. In terms of the assessment of ICC, this approach would mean the testing of each *savoir* separately, perhaps each objective within each *savoir*, using techniques where there was little or no room for disagreement among assessors about the evidence for learners' different skills and knowledge.

The problem with this approach in general is that it atomises knowledge and abilities and does not reflect the dependency relationships between component parts. It does not reflect how individuals use their knowledge and abilities nor the psychological reality for the individuals concerned. With respect to the five *savoirs* of ICC, the problem would be similar: there would be no reflection of the interdependence among the five *savoirs* and linguistic, sociolinguistic and discourses competences. Yet this interdependence is a crucial part of the definition of each competence and the *savoirs* within intercultural competence. The psychological reality of ICC would not be adequately represented in this approach to assessment either; the experience of communicating and interacting in interculturally competent ways is difficult to describe in its complexity and would certainly not be described by isolated tests. As suggested in the previous section, where I attempted to identify means of assessing each *savoir*, the evidence provided from a learner's work on a text or interaction with a person would be attributable to more than one *savoir* or competence.

As a consequence of this kind of problem, there has been a general shift of interest to 'performance assessment', in which knowledge and abilities are evaluated as they are used and evident in activities which might be an application of what has been learnt. Since this kind of evidence is complex and can seldom be quantified in terms of component parts, it is usually assessed against descriptions of what is satisfactory performance (criterion-referenced). In this perspective progression need not be defined as increasing, quantifiable acquisition of knowledge and abilities on a linear scale. Instead, there is also the possibility of defining progression in terms of different kinds of acquisition of knowledge and abilities, 'completing the jigsaw' to use my earlier analogy for curriculum planning. Progression from one criterion to another would involve a qualitative rather than a quantitative change, a move to a different skill for example.

With respect to ICC, progression in this approach might mean that *savoir comprendre* is described in terms of different kinds of understanding of other people's practices. Progression from one to the other, to a stage closer to what is defined as *savoir comprendre* for the intercultural speaker, does not depend on an increase in quantity of knowledge but rather on a leap in insight. In Byram, Morgan *et al.* (1994: 150) we suggested that there is a parallel with ways of assessing historical empathy. We quoted Shemilt (1984) who suggests four levels of empathetic and pre-empathetic understanding:

(1) no valid application of historical or empathetic understanding;
(2) valid historical analysis but 'from the outside'; no evidence of empathetic understanding;
(3) explanation 'from the inside' but only *everyday empathy* ... locked in a twentieth century world view;

(4) genuine historical empathy ... attempt to shed twentieth century preconceptions and to recreate an alien world-view.

The different stages can be seen as several thresholds marking different kinds of understanding. Gipps (1994: 25) cites a distinction made in cognitive science between novices and experts:

> they differ from each other not just in terms of quantity, that is the extent of their knowledge, but also in the types of models they have constructed for themselves, the types of conceptions and understandings they bring to a problem and the strategies and approaches they use.

I suggested in the previous section that learners might provide their own evidence and evaluation of, for example, *savoir faire*, because of the difficulties of collecting evidence in real time. The self-analysis required in this might itself be the subject of evaluation by criteria, to establish levels or models, in Gipps' terms, of self-understanding as well as performance in intercultural communication. The difficulty of formulating criteria is however easy to see, as is the accompanying problem of reliable use of the criteria by different assessors in different situations.[4]

Such problems are serious where assessment is done for purposes of accountability and in particular for certification in its usual form. Since certification is usually used as a guarantee that the individual has acquired certain more or less clearly defined knowledge and abilities, differing interpretations of criteria undermine the guarantee. This is all the more the case when there is no specification in the certificate of the guaranteed knowledge and abilities to accompany the certificate. The gate-keeping function of certification does not require evidence of knowledge and abilities, but only confidence in the guarantee.

An alternative perspective arises however when certification is uncoupled from its function in accountability procedures and gate-keeping and when certification is seen as a means of documenting an individual's knowledge and abilities. The most comprehensive form this might take is the portfolio, in which learners keep evidence and evaluations thereof collected by themselves and their teachers. That evidence could be classified according to the various competences and *savoirs*, with some evidence contributing to the attestation of more than one of these, and to the interdependency of all of them. The portfolio could of course also include test results of a traditional kind where separate components of competences — notably linguistic competence — can be reasonably assessed by objective tests. These would doubtless continue to be the main evidence consulted by the gate-keepers of education and employment but such people could not ignore the existence of other evidence, and its significance in the prediction of performance, of the learner's *savoir faire* in intercultural communication.

At this point the validity of the evidence is seen to be more important than reliability understood as uniformity of evaluation by different assessors. Reliability in a second sense — the assumption that learners will perform equally well each time they are assessed or, more importantly, each time they apply their knowledge and abilities in the future — is also of importance to those who accept the evidence of the portfolio. The validity of the portfolio — the degree to which it embodies ICC — and the reliability of predictions of equal performance on every occasion — are closely related. In addition, there remains the question of the *level* of performance.

Assessing Levels of Intercultural Communicative Competence

In the discussion in Chapter 4 of the concept of a threshold level for ICC, I suggested that several factors should be considered: that a threshold is not a stage on the route to native speaker competence; that the setting of a threshold as a qualification must take pedagogical and motivational issues into account; and that a threshold would be defined according to the environment in which learning is taking place. I pointed out that van Ek's suggestion for a threshold was to set it at a lower level than ideally required in order to give learners an attainable goal, rather than one which seemed distant and out of reach. I further suggested that a threshold can be better defined as the attainable goal of being a competent intercultural speaker in a given situation, rather than a stage on the way to the unattainable goal of native speaker competence.

The discussion in this chapter of assessment of atomised components or of holistic performance of ICC is also relevant to the question of defining a threshold, and other levels below and above. Assessment of separate components could allow a threshold and other levels to be set for each one. The use of a portfolio to document competence allows a combination of atomised and holistic assessment. It also provides the means of maintaining a close relationship between testing and teaching since some documentation would be chosen from the teaching and learning process. A portfolio would therefore allow levels to be set for each component and for holistic performance, with criteria specifying levels of attainment appropriately for each competence and *savoir*. A portfolio also allows a combination of criterion-referenced documentation with objective, norm-referenced tests if this is thought desirable, for example where the portfolio is to be used as a passport to further education opportunities. A portfolio might thus contain: examination certificates and a specification of the linguistic skills examined; a copy of an audio-recording and commentary in which the learner has interviewed someone in the foreign language about a their understanding of the political system and/or their own social identities and socialisation; a reflective account of the learner's experience of a visit to a country where the language is spoken natively; a reflective account of an occasion when the learner had to act as guide and interpreter to a visitor to their own institution; the content and results of a test of the learner's factual knowledge of the history and /or contemporary events of a country whose language they are learning; an example of an annotated translation from the foreign language with the teacher/assessor's evaluation; a linguistic and cultural curriculum vitae describing the learner's experience both within and outside formal learning. The curriculum vitae would be the organising document, allowing the reader of the portfolio to see the biographical progression in ICC, and the relationship of other documents to each other.

Let us consider the nature of a threshold and associated levels for each *savoir*. Although attitude measurement is well developed in the social sciences (Oppenheim, 1992), the definition of *savoir être* in terms of 'willingness', 'readiness', 'interest' and the ability to act accordingly, does not fit well with attitude scales. This is partly because the specifications suggested in Chapter 3 are not simply attitudinal — dispositions to act, 'I would do ...', if the opportunity arose — and the kinds of assessment exercise suggested in this chapter require a shift of perspective, not a movement along a scale. This being the case, the notion of threshold relates to the existence or absence of perspective shift, rather than to a definition of a critical point on a scale. On the other hand, learners may be able to shift perspective on some occasions but not all, and progress could then be defined in terms of frequency of perspective shift. Whalley (1997) offers a theory of perspective shift in cultural learning which could be the basis of a system of evaluation.

Establishing levels for knowledge/*savoirs* is less problematic. It is possible to quantify the knowledge retained from a course or the knowledge acquired at a given point on a given topic. The decision to include a topic in assessment would have to be taken on grounds of learners' predicted needs and/or a rationale for what are central issues and topics in the knowledge of a society and its cultural practices. Since I suggested that 'deep learning' needs to be assessed by techniques such as essay-writing, levels in this case would be determined by criterion-referencing. On the other hand, it is difficult to envisage a definition of a threshold for knowledge unless learners' predicted needs could be defined very precisely, when a threshold in absolute terms would mean mastery of the knowledge so defined. On the other hand, in pedagogical and motivational terms the threshold would be set as a function of the learning time available and take account of short- and medium-term goals as well as the absolute threshold.

The objectives for skill of interpreting and relating (*savoir comprendre*), it was suggested earlier, can be assessed in connection with the assessment of *savoirs* and *savoir faire*. Where the emphasis is upon identifying perspectives and the sources of dysfunctions or misunderstandings, the level of success can be measured in terms of how comprehensive the interpretation of a document or an event has been. Criteria would thus involve a degree of quantification, although precise measurement is unlikely to be possible. Where *savoir comprendre* includes mediation in real time, and is linked to *savoir faire*, a threshold can be defined as the satisfactory resolution of a problem or misunderstanding, that is, satisfactory to those concerned. This is therefore a pragmatic evaluation. Criteria to determine levels above or below the threshold could include reference to the speed of the resolution. Such criteria would not include precise measurement. It is also the case here, as with *savoir être*, that learners might be assessed on the frequency of success, documented over time, since the complexity of mediation processes militates against the possibility of assessing *savoir comprendre* on one occasion only.

The same argument is relevant for *savoir faire* (and that part of *savoir s'engager* which is to be assessed with *savoir faire*). There is no guarantee that success on one occasion means success on a later occasion, which might be more complex. The situation is made more difficult because *savoir faire* is probably best assessed through analysis of performance by the learners themselves, retrospectively. It is extremely demanding to ask the learner to reflect on the degree of complexity of the interaction in order to determine a level of success against a criterion-description of a threshold. Documentation of frequency of success remains the only practical option.

Finally, *savoir apprendre* is parallel to *savoir comprendre* in that the degree of success of identifying significant references or using sources or interactions with native speakers to identify significant references in an event or document, can be assessed in terms of the degree of comprehensiveness of the learner's explanations and interpretations. The assessor would need to determine which references are crucial to understanding and which are complementary. The threshold performance would therefore be a satisfactory interpretation and explanation of the crucial references. Inclusion of complementary references would be deemed better than satisfactory. Again the issue is how comprehensive the interpretation is, as with *savoir comprendre*, but with the requirement that the learner be able to cope with data which is new to them. Clearly, one document or event can include both familiar and new data so that some of the objectives of both *savoir apprendre* and *savoir comprendre* can be identified and assessed within the same performance. On the other hand, it is also possible to isolate objectives for assessment purposes by giving the learner specific data, separately or within a document or event, to which they have to pay particular attention. The degree of difficulty of the task would be dependent on the complexity of the data and the location and frequency of occurrence.

Conclusion

I referred earlier to Gipps' distinction between accountability assessment and educational assessment. Her characterisation of the latter corresponds to many of the approaches to assessment which I have suggested here. This similarity is due in part to my agreement with her stance on assessment, in part to my view that the development of ICC is an *educational* process, and in part to the nature of the competences I have been considering. It seems to me inevitable that, once the objectives and specifications have been defined as they were in Chapters 2 and 3, the forms of assessment follow logically from them. The cultural dimension of ICC — as opposed to linguistic, sociolinguistic and discourse competence — is inseparably linked with educational values, as well as having pragmatic and skill-based significance. In this sense, traditional claims that language learning has educational value are borne out in the acquisition of the knowledge, skills and attitudes of intercultural competence.

Gipps' (1994: 159–161) summary of educational assessment includes the following:

- educational assessment recognises that domains and constructs are multi-dimensional and complex (this is clearly the case with intercultural competence)
- clear standards are set for performance against which pupils will be assessed; these and assessment processes are shared with pupils; pupils are encouraged to monitor and reflect on their own work/performance so that they become self-monitoring learners (we have seen the need to involve learners in the assessment of their ICC, particularly those aspects which can only be documented from real-time interaction and retrospectively)
- assessment criteria are more holistic than in criterion-referenced assessment as originally conceived, to allow for the assessment of complex skills (I have suggested that criteria will need to refer to

degrees of success in dealing comprehensively with a task, as well as identifying specific details of *savoirs* or particular references to be illuminated by *savoir comprendre* or *savoir apprendre*)
- in educational assessment we move away from the notion of a score, a single statistic, and look at other forms of describing achievement including 'thick' description of achievement and profiles of performance (it has become clear that some aspects of ICC can only be documented over time and by the collection of descriptive information in a portfolio).

One important aspect of all assessment is its effect upon teaching and learning. When both teachers and learners can see that complex competences are assessed in complex ways, they are reassured in the pursuit of their objectives. It is the simplification of competences to what can be 'objectively' tested which has a detrimental effect: the learning of trivial facts, the reduction of subtle understanding to generalisations and stereotypes, the lack of attention to interaction and engagement because these are not tested. When assessment recognises all aspects of ICC, even if they cannot be quantified and reduced to a single score, then the learner can see their efforts rewarded, and the teacher and curriculum planner can give full attention to the whole phenomenon of ICC rather than only that which can be represented statistically.

Notes

1. This is just one, but the most visible, of the advantages I have found in working interculturally and inter-lingually with Geneviève Zarate in recent years and I would like to state again my indebtedness to her.
2. In an account of the genre of 'toasting' in Georgia, Kotthoff (1996) describes how foreigners are expected not to attempt to follow the conventions of long and complex toasts but to contribute a toast which is that of an outsider. She also demonstrates how, on one occasion, she could not accept a toast to the reunification of Germany which was intended as a compliment, thus creating a tension in relationships which had to be resolved to the satisfaction of both sides.
3. A similar situation exists in Germany where teachers examine their students' work on the basis of professional judgement, (HMI, 1986).
4. Where the ambition is to establish criteria for use internationally as with the Council of Europe's (1996) Framework of reference for language learning and teaching, the difficulties are compounded by translation. Establishing a common understanding of criteria is crucial to reliability and difficult enough with assessors who share a native language. If they are using criteria in a foreign language or translated from a foreign language the problems are obviously much increased.

Conclusion

I do not propose in this conclusion to summarise. I hope there has been sufficient repetition of the general argument and of specific points about ICC from chapter to chapter to make a summary superfluous. Furthermore the significance of the argument and of my proposals has to stand or fall by the detail in which I have worked through the consequences for curriculum and assessment of the concept of ICC. I do not intend to repeat the general terms.

Intercultural Communicative Competence and Lingua Franca

There is however one issue which requires further discussion: the question of ICC and the use of a language as a lingua franca. I have mentioned this from time to time by discussing the consequences of two intercultural speakers of a language interacting and knowing little or nothing about the cultural beliefs, meanings and behaviours of the other. In many cases, they will have studied and interacted with native speakers, and that may be the only common ground they have. On the other hand, it might be suggested that where it is known that learners will use a language mainly or even exclusively as a lingua franca, study of the cultures of native speakers is not necessary. This argument is supported by those who fear that, particularly in the teaching of English, there is a danger of neo-colonialism, as American and western values in general are imported with the language (Phillipson, 1992; Pennycook, 1994). The strength of feeling about this is evident in the extract from the statement of aims of education in Qatar already mentioned in Chapter 1. It is clear that such countries feel a strong need for English as a lingua franca (Elf) — for the technological advances it can bring, for example — but fear the influences it may bring with it. On the other hand it is worth noting that Elf can also serve a cultural mission in the opposite direction, and it is recognised that through study of another culture that one becomes more aware of one's own.

A concrete formulation of the general question is therefore whether ICC in Elf should be defined differently. The first point to note is that by replacing the native speaker by the intercultural speaker as a model for learners, the implication that they should submit themselves to the values of the native speaker and try to imitate native speaker behaviours just as they imitate a native speaker standard grammar and pronunciation disappears. Imitation is replaced by comparison, establishing a relationship between one's own beliefs, meanings and behaviours and those of the other, whoever that happens to be. Furthermore, as noted in the example from Qatar, it is through comparison that one becomes more aware of one's own culture, much of which is unconscious and taken-for-granted. This can therefore support rather than threaten one's cultural identity:

> The characteristics of one's group as a whole (such as its status, its richness or its poverty, its skin colour or its ability to reach its aims) achieve most of their significance in relation to perceived differences from other groups and the value connotations of these differences (...) the definition of a group (national or racial or any other) makes no sense unless there are other groups around. (Tajfel, 1978: 66)

The emphasis in ICC on the acquisition of skills and attitudes as well as knowledge is compatible with Elf since they involve learners in questioning and discovering, not in simply accepting a transmitted account of a specific country and its dominant culture, which might be feared by less powerful countries. *Savoir apprendre* and *savoir comprendre* are more likely to instil a doubting rather than an accepting attitude, which should be counter-balanced by the openness and willingness to suspend disbelief in other views and unthinking belief in one's own, *savoir être*. It is clear therefore that ICC encourages a critical as well as open approach to otherness but also towards oneself and one's cultural beliefs, meanings and behaviours.

It is not a question of doubt and criticism merely for its own sake. The inclusion in ICC of *savoir s'engager*/critical cultural awareness as an educational aim for foreign language teaching is crucial. The purpose here is to ensure that a critical stance is based on a clearly articulated set of beliefs, even though these are not simply and blindly accepted but are themselves open to comparison with otherness. In that sense ICC serves the Qatari purpose of spreading a better understanding of 'one's own religion, culture, and values and to influence world public opinion favourably towards one's people and their causes'. On the other hand it is clear that one's own religion, culture and values come under scrutiny in intercultural interactions, and that the intercultural speaker reflects upon their own as much as upon the other's.

The area which remains is that of knowledge/*savoirs*. The traditional study of English focused on Britain would put much emphasis on the acquisition of factual information about British life and institutions. Since it is clear that such information is not neutral, and since the information was not put into a critical frame, the implication that the values implicit in the information were being promoted surreptitiously is quickly and justifiably inferred. On the other hand, the critical study of the same British life and institutions within a critical framework can be a challenging educational programme, as is evident from recent developments in British Cultural Studies (e.g. Bassnett, 1997) The educational purpose of helping learners, in this case adult learners at an advanced stage of study, to reflect upon and critique the beliefs, meanings and behaviours of British cultures, and not simply the one dominant culture, is an example of critical cultural awareness/*savoir s'engager*. Such programmes do not however give as much emphasis to a comparative and relational study of British cultures and their own.[1]

It could still be argued that the intercultural speaker of Elf does not need even this critical approach to British Studies, or the study of any other English-speaking country. In the Qatari and similar cases, young learners are taught English from textbooks where the main focus is on topics from their own country, with minimal, often stereotype representation of Britain, which only reinforces their existing perceptions. The problem with this approach is that it does not provide a basis on which to develop the skills of *savoir comprendre* and *savoir apprendre*, and there is no possibility of relating one's own to the other, still less of gaining a critical perspective on both. It is also clear from such situations that there has to be some content to language learning, and it is argued with respect to immersion programmes that the more attention there is on the content, the better the learning.

This suggests another option: that learning of English should take its content from other areas of the curriculum, and English become the medium of instruction. It is possible to envisage a methodology based on immersion-type programmes, where alternatives are presented and the potential for comparison of one's own pre-suppositions and those of another culture created. For example, learners studying the history curriculum through English would be introduced not only to the national curriculum of their country for history but would study alternative interpretations of the same event. They would thus be acquiring general relational and relativising knowledge through a specific example, which would of course inevitably include a critical reflection on that which in their own society is taken for granted as 'historical truth'. Not all curriculum areas lend themselves so well to this approach — others that do are geography and social studies — but neither is it necessary that it be constantly present.

In short, the crucial element of the knowledge/*savoirs* dimension is that it should include a comparative method and be related to the development of critical cultural awareness/*savoir s'engager*. Thereafter the decision about what should be the focus, whether an English-speaking country or not, is less significant. The advantages of focusing on an English-speaking country where English is the subject rather than the medium for other subjects, is that western — especially American and British — cultures are so dominant even where learners will have no need or opportunity to interact with native speakers, that a *critical* study of them and their relationship to learners' own is likely to be more beneficial than to ignore their presence. It thus seems to me that the acquisition of intercultural communicative competence can take place through the learning of a lingua franca, whether English or another language, just as it can through more traditional forms of foreign language learning.

'Foreign' Language Learning

Finally, I would like to return to the phrase 'foreign language learning'. The identification of issues specific to a lingua franca could be paralleled with discussion of other varieties of language learning. As I said in the introduction, the distinctions for example between 'second' and 'foreign' are questions of degree rather than dichotomy, and whatever the terminology, language teaching has to be planned and evaluated with respect to particular contexts. There is a further difficulty with the term 'foreign language learning' and that is the way in which it turns attention outwards and away from the learner's own language and culture. It will be clear that introducing the concept of *inter*cultural speaker runs counter to this traditional focus of attention, because the intercultural speaker is positioned precisely between the foreign and their own language and culture. In a similar way, the phrase 'foreign language teaching' is unsatisfactory because it ignores the educational value of language learning, and I prefer the phrase 'foreign language education' (see Byram, 1989a).

All this is encapsulated in the words of the anthropologist Peter Winch, which I will amend slightly to ensure that the unity of language-and-culture learning is not lost:

> What we may learn by studying other cultures (-and-languages, I would add) are not merely possibilities of different ways of doing things, other techniques. More importantly we may learn different possibilities of making sense of human life, different ideas about the possible importance that the carrying out of certain activities may take on for a (person) trying to contemplate the sense of (their) life as a whole. (Winch, 1964:321)

Notes

1. But see Husemann (1994), for an example of how a comparative approach is central to one programme.

References

Abu Jalalah, F. (1993) The cultural dimension of teaching English as a foreign language in an Arab Gulf State. Unpublished PhD thesis, University of Durham.

Al-Hail, A. (1995) The teaching of media studies: A study in theory and practice. Unpublished PhD thesis, University of Durham.

Alix, C. and Bertrand, G. (eds.) (1994) *Pour une pédagogie des échanges* (*Le français dans le monde, numéro spécial*). Paris: EDICEF.

Allport, G. (1979) *The Nature of Prejudice*. Reading MA: Addison-Wesley.

Argyle, M. (1983) *The Psychology of Interpersonal Behaviour*. Harmondsworth: Penguin (4th edition).

Bachmann, S. *et al.* (1995) *Sichtwechsel neu*. Stuttgart: Ernst Klett Verlag.

Barro, A., Jordan, S. and Roberts, C. (in press) Cultural practice in everyday life: The language learner as ethnographer. In M. Byram and M. Fleming (eds.) *Language Learning in Intercultural Perspective*. Cambridge: Cambridge University Press.

Barth, F. (1969) Introduction. *Ethnic Groups and Boundaries*. London: Allen and Unwin.

Bassnett, S. (ed.) *Studying British Cultures: An Introduction*. London: Routledge.

Becher, U.A.J. (1996) European citizenship and historical learning. *Evaluation and Research in Education* 10 (2&3), 79–87.

Behal-Thomsen, H. *et al.* (1993) *Typisch deutsch? Arbeitsbuch zu Aspekten deutscher Mentalität*. Berlin: Langenscheidt.

Berger, P.L. and Luckmann, T. (1966) *The Social Construction of Reality*. Harmondsworth: Penguin.

Bourdieu, P. (1989) *La Noblesse d'Etat*. Paris: Minuit.

Bourdieu, P. (1990) *In Other Words: Essays Towards a Reflexive Sociology*. New York: Polity Press.

Brecht, R.D. and Walton, A.R. (1995) The future shape of language learning in the new world of global communication: Consequences for higher education and beyond. In R. Donato and R.M. Terry (eds.) *Foreign Language Learning: The Journey of a Lifetime*. Lincolnwood: National Textbook Company.

Bulletin of the European Communities (1988), no. 5.

Byram, M. (1978) New objectives in language teaching. *Modern Languages* 59 (4), 204–207.

Byram, M. (1979) Performance objectives and language teaching. *Modern Languages* 60 (2), 111–115.

Byram, M. (1989a) *Cultural Studies in Foreign Language Education*. Clevedon: Multilingual Matters.

Byram, M. (1989b) Intercultural education and foreign language teaching. *World Studies Journal* 7 (2), 4–7.

Byram, M. (ed.) (1993) *Germany: Its Representation in Textbooks for Teaching German in Great Britain*. Frankfurt/Main: Diesterweg.

Byram, M. (ed.) (1994) *Culture and Language Learning in Higher Education*. Clevedon: Multilingual Matters.

Byram, M. (1997a) Cultural studies and foreign language teaching. In S. Bassnett (ed.) *Studying British Cultures: An Introduction*. London: Routledge.
Byram, M. (ed.) (1997b) *Face to Face: Learning Language and Culture through Visits and Exchanges*. London: Centre for Information on Language Teaching and Research.
Byram, M. (in press a) 'Cultural awareness' through vocabulary learning. *Language Learning Journal*.
Byram, M. (in press b) Source disciplines for language teacher education. *Papers from the 4th IALS Symposium*. New York: Prentice Hall.
Byram, M., Morgan, C. *et al.* (1994) *Teaching-and-Learning Language-and-Culture*. Clevedon: Multilingual Matters.
Byram, M. and Zarate, G. (1994) *Definitions, Objectives and Assessment of Socio-cultural Objectives*. Strasbourg: Council of Europe.
Byram, M. and Zarate, G. (1995) *Young People Facing Difference*. Strasbourg: Council of Europe.
Byram, M. and Zarate, G. (1997) Defining and assessing intercultural competence: Some principles and proposals for the European context. *Language Teaching* 29, 14–18.
Campos, C. *et al.* (1988) *L'enseignement de la civilisation française dans les universités de l'Europe*. Paris: Didier Erudition.
Canale, M. and Swain, M. (1980) Theoretical bases of communicative approaches to second language teaching and testing. *Applied Linguistics* 1 (1), 1–47.
Christensen, J.G. (1993) New paradigms in cultural studies? From culture to theories of practice. Paper given at a conference on Cross-cultural Understanding in a Foreign Language Perspective. University of Roskilde, October 1993.
Christensen, J.G. (1994) Sprog og kultur i europæisk integration. In J. Liep and K.F. Olwig (eds) *Komplekse liv. Kulturel mangfoldighed i Danmark*. Copenhagen: Akademisk Forlag.
Classen-Bauer, I. (1989) *International Understanding through Foreign Language Teaching*. Bonn: Deutsche UNESCO Kommission.
Council of Europe, 1993 Transparency and coherence in language learning in Europe: Objectives, assessment and certification. Report on the Ruschlikon Symposium. CC LANG (19) 22.
Council of Europe (1996) *Common European Framework of Reference for Language Learning and Teaching*. Strasbourg: Council of Europe.
Cummins, J. (1984) *Bilingualism and Special Education: Issues in Assessment and Pedagogy*. Clevedon: Multilingual Matters.
Dark, S. *et al.* (1997) The study visit: An opportunity for culture learning. In M. Byram (ed.) *Face to Face: Learning Language and Culture through Visits and Exchanges*. London: Centre for Information on Language Teaching and Research.
Dirven, R. and Putz, M. (1993) Intercultural communication. *Language Teaching* 26, 144–156.
Doyé, P. (1991) *Großbritannien: seine Darstellung in deutschen Schulbüchern für den Englischunterricht*. Frankfurt/Main: Diesterweg.
Doyé, P. (1993) Neuere Konzepte der Fremdsprachenerziehung und ihre Bedeutung für die Schulbuchkritik. In M. Byram (ed.) *Germany: Its Representation in Textbooks for Teaching German in Great Britain*. Frankfurt/Main: Diesterweg.
DES (1990) *Modern Foreign Languages in the National Curriculum*. London: HMSO.
Ertelt-Vieth, A. (1991) Culture and 'hidden culture' in Moscow: A contrastive analysis of West German and Soviet perceptions. In D. Buttjes and M. Byram

(eds) *Mediating Languages and Cultures: Towards an Intercultural Theory of Foreign Language Education*. Clevedon: Multilingual Matters.
European Commission (1996) *Teaching and Learning: Towards the Learning Society*. Brussels: European Commission.
Fairclough, N. (1989) *Language and Power*. Harlow: Longman.
Francesconi, M. and di Fasano, D.S. (1994) L'échange à part soi: un point de vue psychanalytique sur une expérience d'échange linguistique. In C. Alix and G. Bertrand (eds) *Pour une pédagogie des échanges* (*Le français dans le monde: numéro special*). Paris: EDICEF.
Furnham, A. and Bochner, S. (1986) *Culture Shock: Psychological Reactions in Unfamiliar Environments*. London: Methuen.
Gagel, W. (1983) *Einführung in die Didaktik des politischen Unterrichts*. Opladen: Leske and Budrich.
Geertz, C. (1975) *The Interpretation of Cultures*. London: Hutchinson.
Gipps, C. (1994) *Beyond Testing: Towards a Theory of Educational Assessment*. London: Falmer Press.
Gudykunst, W.B. (1994) *Bridging Differences: Effective Intergroup Communication* (2nd edn). London: Sage.
Hawkins, E. (1987) *Modern Languages in the Curriculum* (2nd edn). Cambridge: Cambridge University Press.
HMI (Her Majesty's Inspectorate) (1986) *Education in the Federal Republic of Germany: Aspects of Curriculum Development and Assessment*. London: HMSO.
Holec, H. (1980) *Autonomie et apprentissage des langues étrangers*. Strasbourg: Council of Europe.
Husemann, H. (1994) From NIMBY Landeskunde to IMBY cultural studies. In M. Byram (ed.) *Culture and Language Learning in Higher Education*. Clevedon: Multilingual Matters.
Hyland, T. (1993) Competence, knowledge and education. *Journal of Philosophy of Education* 27 (1), 57–68.
Hymes, D. (1972) On communicative competence. In J.B. Pride and J. Holmes (eds) *Sociolinguistics*. Harmondsworth: Penguin.
Jæger, K. (1995) Teaching culture: State of the art. In L. Sercu (ed.) *Intercultural Competence: A New Challenge for Language Teachers and Trainers in Europe*. Aalborg: Aalborg University Press.
Jones, B. (1995) *Exploring Otherness: An Approach to Cultural Awareness*. London: CILT.
Kasper, G. (1995) Wessen Pragmatik? Für eine Neubestimmung fremdsprachlicher Handlungskompetenz. *Zeitschrift für Fremdsprachenforschung* 6, 69–94.
Kim. Y.Y. (1988) *Communication and Cross-cultural Adaptations: An Integrative Theory*. Clevedon: Multilingual Matters.
Knapp, K. and Knapp-Potthoff, A. (1990) Interkulturelle Kommunikation. *Zeitschrift für Fremdsprachenforschung* 1, 62–93.
Kohlberg, L., Levine, C. and Hewer, A. (1983) *Moral Stages: A Current Formulation and Response to Critics*. Basel: Karger.
Kolb, D.A. (1984) *Experiential Learning*. Englewood Cliffs: Prentice Hall.
Kotthoff, H. (1996) Georgian toasts and the limits of cross-cultural accommodation: Perspectives on the interrelation of speech genres and culture. In E. Ambos and I. Werner (eds) *Interkulturelle Dimensionen der Fremdsprachenkompetenz*. Bochum: AKS-Verlag.

Kramsch, C. (1993) *Context and Culture in Language Teaching*. Oxford: Oxford University Press.

Kramsch, C. (in press) The privilege of the intercultural speaker. In M. Byram and M. Fleming (eds) *Language Learning in Intercultural Perspective*. Cambridge: Cambridge University Press.

Kramsch, C. (1993) Language study as border study: Experiencing difference. *European Journal of Education* 28 (3), 349–358.

Le Page, R.B. and Tabouret-Keller, A. (1985) *Acts of Identity*. Cambridge: Cambridge University Press.

Leblanc, C., Courtel, C. and Trescases, P. (1990) *Etude nationale sur les programmes de base*. Ottawa: Assoc. Canadienne des Professeurs de Langues Secondes.

Leblanc, R. (1990) *Etude nationale sur les programmes de français de base. Rapport de synthèse*. Ottawa: Assoc. Canadienne des Professeurs de Langues Secondes.

Mebus, G. *et al.* (1987) *Sprachbrücke. Deutsch als Fremdsprache*. Stuttgart: Ernst Klett Verlag.

Melde, W. (1987) *Zur Integration von Landeskunde und Kommunikation im Fremdsprachenunterricht*. Tubingen: Gunter Narr Verlag.

Meyer, M. (1991) Developing transcultural competence: Case studies of advanced foreign language learners. In D. Buttjes and M. Byram (eds) *Mediating Languages and Cultures: Towards a Theory of Foreign Language Education*. Clevedon: Multilingual Matters.

McPartland, M., Semple, J. and Byram, M. (1996) Olomouc and Durham: An interdisciplinary curriculum project. Paper given at the British Studies conference, Prague, October 1996.

Nunan, D. (1988) *The Learner-centred Curriculum*. Cambridge: Cambridge University Press.

O'Keefe, B.J. and Delia, G.J. (1985) Psychological and interactional dimensions of communicative development. In H. Giles and R.N. St. Clair (eds) *Recent Advances in Language Communication and Social Psychology*. London: Lawrence Erlbaum.

Oppenheim, A.N. (1992) *Questionnaire Design, Interviewing and Attitude Measurement*. London: Pinter.

Paulston, C.B. (1992) *Sociolinguistic Perspectives on Bilingual Education*. Clevedon: Multilingual Matters.

Pennycook, A. (1994) *The Cultural Politics of English as an International Language*. London: Longman.

Phillipson, R. (1992) *Linguistic Imperialism*. Oxford: Oxford University Press.

Poulain, R. (1997) Training for encounter and encounter for training. In M. Byram (ed.) *Face to Face: Learning Language and Culture through Visits and Exchanges*. London: Centre for Information on Language Teaching and Research.

Poyatos, F. (1992) Non-verbal communication in foreign language teaching: Theoretical and methodological perspectives. In A. Helbo (ed.) *Evaluation and Language Teaching*. Bern: Peter Lang.

Poyatos, F. (1993) *Paralanguage: A Linguistic and Interdisciplinary Approach to Interactive Speech and Sound*. Amsterdam: John Benjamins.

Roberts, C. (forthcoming) *Language Learners as Ethnographers: Introducing Cultural Processes into Advanced Language Learning*.

Roulet, E. (1977) *Un Niveau-Seuil. Présentation et guide d'emploi*. Strasbourg: Council of Europe.

Ruben, B.D. (1989) The study of cross-cultural competence: Traditions and contemporary issues. *International Journal of Intercultural Relations* 13, 229–240.
Ryle, G. (1949) *The Concept of Mind*. London: Hutchinson.
Salvadori, E. (1997) Taking language beyond the classroom. In M. Byram (ed.) *Face to Face: Learning Language and Culture through Visits and Exchanges*. London: Centre for Information on Language Teaching and Research.
Sercu, L. (1995) The acquisition of intercultural competence. A teacher training seminar. In L. Sercu (ed.) *Intercultural Competence, Vol. I: The Secondary School*. Aalborg: Aalborg University Press.
Shemilt, D. (1984) Beauty and the philosopher: Empathy in history and the classroom. In A.K. Dickinson *et al*. (eds.) *Learning History*. London: Heinemann.
Singerman, A.J. (1996) *Acquiring Cross-cultural Competence: Four Stages for American Students of French*. Lincolnwood, IL: National Textbook Company.
Snow, D. and Byram, M. (in press) *Crossing Frontiers: The Study Visit Abroad*. London: Centre for Information on Language Teaching and Research.
Standards for Foreign Language Learning: Preparing for the 21st Century (1996) Yonkers, NY: National Standards in Foreign Language Education Project.
Starkey, H. (1988) Foreign languages and global education. In G. Pike and D. Selbey (eds) *Global Teacher, Global Learner*. London: Hodder and Stoughton.
Starkey H. (1995) Intercultural education through foreign language learning: A human rights approach. In A. Osler *et al*. (eds) *Teaching for Citizenship in Europe*. Stoke-on-Trent: Trentham Books.
Stern, H.H. (1983) *Fundamental Concepts in Language Teaching*. Oxford: Oxford University Press.
Street, B. (1993) Culture is a verb. In D. Graddol *et al*. (eds) *Language and Culture*. Clevedon: Multilingual Matters.
Tajfel, H. (ed.) (1978) *Differentiation Between Social Groups*. London: Academic Press.
Tajfel, H. (1981) *Human Groups and Social Categories*. Cambridge: Cambridge University Press.
Trim, J.L.M. (1978) *Developing a Unit/Credit Scheme of Adult Language Learning*. Oxford: Pergamon Press.
Trim, J.L.M. (1996) Personal communication.
van Ek, J.A. (1980) The 'threshold level' in a unit/credit system. In J.L.M. Trim *et al*. (eds) *Systems Development in Adult Language Learning*. Oxford: Pergamon.
van Ek, J.A. (1986) *Objectives for Foreign Language Learning, Vol. 1: Scope*. Strasbourg: Council of Europe.
van Ek, J. and Trim, J.L.M. (1991) *Threshold Level 1990*. Strasbourg: Council of Europe.
van Ek, J. and Trim, J.L.M. (1996) *Vantage Level*. Strasbourg: Council of Europe (internal document).
Vivian, J. and Brown, R. (1995) Prejudice and intergroup conflict. In M. Argyle and A.M. Cohen (eds) *Social Psychology* (pp. 57–77). London: Longman.
Whalley, T. (1997) Culture learning as transformative learning. In M. Byram (ed.) *Face to Face: Learning Language-and-Culture through Visits and Exchanges*. London: Centre for Information on Language Teaching (CILT).
Winch, P. (1964) Understanding a primitive society. *American Philosophical Quarterly* 1 (4), 307–324.
Zarate, G., Murphy-Lejeune, E. and Byram, M. (eds) (1996) *Cultural Representations in Language Learning and Teacher Training. Special issue of Language, Culture and Curriculum* 9 (1), 1996.

Index

Lightning Source UK Ltd.
Milton Keynes UK
UKOW031950110113

204783UK00001B/4/A